SYDNEY THEN & NOW

Telstra
ING DIRECT
Allianz
AQUARIUM

SYDNEY THEN & NOW

CAROLINE MACKANESS
AND
CAROLINE BUTLER-BOWDON

THUNDER BAY
P·R·E·S·S
San Diego, California

Thunder Bay Press
An imprint of the Advantage Publishers Group
5880 Oberlin Drive, San Diego, CA 92121-4794
www.thunderbaybooks.com

Produced by PRC Publishing
151 Freston Road
London W10 6TH, United Kingdom

An imprint of Anova Books Company Ltd

All notations of errors or omissions should be addressed to Thunder Bay Press, Editorial Department, at the above address. All other correspondence (author inquiries, permissions) concerning the content of this book should be addressed to PRC Publishing, 151 Freston Road, London W10 6TH, United Kingdom. An imprint of Anova Books Company Ltd.

ISBN-13: 978-1-59223-551-3
ISBN-10: 1-59223-551-4

Printed and bound in China

2 3 4 5 09 08 07 06

ACKNOWLEDGMENTS
The authors would like to extend their thanks to the Historic Houses Trust of NSW who supported the exhibition project, Sydney @ Federation, which formed the basis of research for the 'then' text and photographs, and Nicola Teffer for her research assistance on this exhibition project.

The Historic Houses Trust is a statutory authority which conserves, manages and interprets important properties and house museums in New South Wales for the education and enjoyment of the public. Properties of the Trust include: Elizabeth Bay House, Elizabeth Farm, Government House, Hyde Park Barracks Museum, Justice & Police Museum, Meroogal, Museum of Sydney on the site of first Government House, Rose Seidler House, Rouse Hill estate, Susannah Place, The Mint and Vaucluse House.

Special thanks to Dr Charles Pickett for the huge contribution in the preparation of text and photographs for the book. Within the staff of the Historic Houses Trust we would like to extend our thanks to Peter Watts and Helen Temple for embracing the project; Robert Griffin for text on a number of HHT properties, Richard Taylor and Louise Ruddock for assistance with some site text; Margaret McAllister and Beth Hise for editorial advice; Scott Carlin, Nerida Campbell, Anna Cossu for sourcing images for individual sites and for facilitation of photography; Ross Heathcote for photography of several key sites; Michelle Andringa for copyright clearance of text; and John Morgan for legal advice. The authors extend their thanks to the following individuals and institutions for assistance with interpretation and photography of individual sites: Anne Flanagan and Steven Miller at the Art Gallery of New South Wales; Margaret Betteridge at the Sydney City Council; Amy Cantrill of the Sydney Cricket and Sports Ground Trust; Shane Moore, Commander, Royal Australian Navy; and Mike Craig of the George Washington Wilson collection.

PICTURE CREDITS:
The publisher wishes to thank the following for kindly supplying the photographs that appear in this book:

Then photographs
Art Gallery of New South Wales, Archives Collection: 138.
Harewood House Trust, Collection of the Justice & Police Museum: 134.
Powerhouse Museum, Sydney: 106, 132. Swain & Liddy Collection, Powerhouse Museum, Sydney: 10, 52, 62, 86, 118. Tyrrell Collection, Powerhouse Museum, Sydney: 1, 8, 12, 14, 16, 18, 20, 22, 24, 30, 32, 34, 36, 38, 40, 42, 44, 46, 48, 50, 54, 56, 60, 66, 70, 72, 78, 80, 82, 84, 92, 94, 96, 98, 102, 104, 108, 110, 112, 116, 120, 122, 124, 126, 128, 130, 136, 140, 142.
State Library of New South Wales, Mitchell Library: 28, 90, 100, 114.
© University of Aberdeen, www.abdn.ac.uk/gww: 6, 26, 58, 64, 68, 74, 76, 88.

Now photographs
All photographs were taken by Simon Clay (© Anova Image Library), with the following exceptions;
© Anova Image Library/Ross Heathcote: 23, 55, 65, 67, 81, 93, 95, 97, 99, 101, 119, 123.

INTRODUCTION

Founded as a colonial outpost and dumping ground for convicts, Sydney has been transformed in the short space of two hundred years into a thriving metropolis set in an unrivalled location. Sydney's identity is inextricably bound by its magnificent harbour —a fingered waterway of beaches, rivers, islands and bays. It was originally home to the Aborigines, who lived at one with the land, fishing from the harbour's shores and travelling in simple bark canoes between the numerous islands and the shore.

When Captain Arthur Phillip planted the Union Jack at Sydney Cove in 1788—taking advantage of its sheltered anchorage, friendly topography and fresh water stream—the landscape and its people were undisturbed. Sydney Cove was the founding site of European settlement in Australia, a place of early hardship, struggle for survival and toil. Transported convicts shaped the land, hewed the rock and carved the early roads. Governor Lachlan Macquarie pursued and shaped an early civic vision for the fledgling colony with the erection of the first significant public buildings such as the Hyde Park Barracks, St. James Church and the Mint—surviving in Sydney still.

The maritime locale shaped both Sydney's foundation and its flourishing growth. Sydney Cove developed as the hub of a trading port, a working harbour with a strong shipbuilding industry and maritime trade. By 1900, Sydney was the fifth largest port in the British Empire, after London, Liverpool, Newcastle and Cardiff. Sydney Cove also became the main terminal for harbour commuter ferries. Today's quay is a bustling focus of transport and pleasure seekers, commuters and tourists, a site of convergence of Sydney's many personalities.

Like all cities, Sydney is composed of layers of lost cities, of urban detail that has survived, been altered, destroyed or built over. Sydney's base stratum is its ramshackle pattern of narrow, crooked streets, created for bullock carts rather than motor vehicles, buses and monorails. Over this Georgian maze, generations of planners, politicians and profiteers have sought to superimpose cities of grand spaces, broad avenues, sandstone palazzi, and steel and glass towers. However, the founding urban pattern has mostly proved resilient and still frames Sydney then and now.

Most of the historic photos in this book catch Sydney scenes of about a century ago, in the decades just before and after the federation of the British colonies to form Australia. Investment in urbanity and public spaces became crucial elements of civic pride and identity. James Barnet, Colonial Architect from 1862 to 1890, created many of Sydney's landmark public buildings, notably the General Post Office, the Colonial Secretary's Office, the Lands Department and the Customs House. Other public buildings erected during this time include the Sydney Town Hall, the much-loved retail building—the Queen Victoria Building, and Central Railway Terminal.

At the turn of the century Sydney was a metropolis facing many urban problems. Shortly after surpassing Melbourne to become the nation's most populous city, Sydney began to confront the modern urban problems of congestion and public squalor. In 1900, bubonic plague broke out in the dockside streets of Millers Point and Darling Harbour, causing the quarantine of the dockside area and 1800 of its residents.

The plague area, including wharves, residential and commercial buildings, was rebuilt. In Sydney's largest public work before the construction of the Harbour Bridge, the waterfront was rebuilt from Circular Quay to the foot of Darling Harbour. The need to deal with planning issues led to the Royal Commission on the Improvement of Sydney and Suburbs of 1908-9, which created a template for modern Sydney, with a focus on major public works such as the city railways, the harbour bridge and modern wharves.

Sydney's major urban aspiration during Victorian times was a harbour bridge or tunnel. There was a great deal of debate concerning the best engineering solution for the meeting of transport modes at Circular Quay and whether it should be underground or overhead. The much-loved Sydney Harbour Bridge was finally built and opened in March 1932 while the less popular Cahill Expressway that now frames and dominates the Quay, was opened in 1958.

The photographs of Sydney today portray a different scene. The Royal Botanic Gardens, the Domain, Hyde Park and Cook and Phillip Parks—established with foresight early in the city's history—cut a swathe of green along Sydney's eastern side, extending from the Opera House at the harbour's edge. Hedged in by this green belt and halted in its eastward spread, the city clusters at the perimeter of the park and gardens, forced to go upward rather than outward in its quest for more space.

The 1960s and 1970s consolidation of city blocks produced a different scale at pedestrian level, however an apartment boom has seen the inner city's population increase for the first time in decades, restoring nightlife and entertainment to the central business district. In a post-Industrial age, wharves and rail yards have abandoned the harbour's edge, now rebuilt as lifestyle and housing precincts. Sydney was revamped for international attention during the 2000 Olympic Games and the start of the new millennium. Today's Sydney faces a new generation of urban challenges.

While there is no disputing the cost of constant city redevelopment, the consequence is not, as is often argued, a cityscape that lacks heritage or pleasure. After two centuries, the diversity of the buildings and people of the city streets combine with a dramatic harbour setting to create a unique metropolis. The book immerses you in the streetscapes, public spaces, harbour life, significant buildings and events of Federation Sydney and the Sydney of the new millennium. In comparing the city and harbour then and now, you can be the judge.

Milsons Point faces Sydney from the north shore of the harbour, making it a favourite spot for artists and photographers. When this photo was taken around 1900, the city skyline was still capped by the clock towers of the Lands Department and the General Post Office. The proximity of Milsons Point to the Quay made it the transport focus of the harbour's north side. Milsons Point wharf was connected to the tramways in 1886, leading to an enormous increase in passengers and consolidating it as a major ferry terminus. The 1893 extension of the North Shore railway line, terminating at the tram and ferry exchange, made Milsons Point the hub of ferry traffic on the north shore before the completion of the Harbour Bridge. The car ferry at Dawes Point, on Sydney Cove's western side, handled ever-increasing traffic to the North Shore, spurring debate about a more efficient transport link.

SYDNEY FROM MILSONS POINT

Milsons Point now occupies the shadow of the Sydney Harbour Bridge. More than any other structure, this massive project transformed Sydney into a modern metropolis. The Bridge linked Sydney's transport system, promoted the expansion of both city and suburbs, gave self-confidence and a new symbol to the city. Today's city skyline is evidence of the transformation. The driving force behind the bridge was J.J.C. Bradfield, Chief Engineer, Sydney Harbour Bridge, who ended decades of debate and inaction with the commencement of construction in 1924. Although argument continues as to the balance of design input between Bradfield and the English construction contractors Dorman Long, to Sydneysiders, the Bridge remains Bradfield's triumph. The opening of the Bridge in 1932, in the depths of the Great Depression, is a celebrated moment of Sydney optimism and pride.

In 1900 most of the north shore was still bush land, but the harbourside suburbs were growing rapidly. The 1900 bubonic plague gave extra impetus to the move to a healthier and less polluted environment. There were water shortages in North Sydney in 1902 as municipal infrastructure struggled to cope with the influx. Suburban living in detached houses was still a novelty in 1910. In this view towards Milsons Point and Kirribilli, most of the residences are terraced row houses, indistinguishable from those of the inner city. But the North Shore rail line, terminating at the Milsons Point ferry wharf, formed the spine of kilometres of new suburbs, each competing for the right combination of privacy and prominence. The large building on the next headland, at Kirribilli, is Beulah (built in 1908), Sydney's first large apartment block and forerunner of another expression of domestic exclusivity.

The view from above the McMahons Point ferry wharf is today dominated by the Harbour Bridge and its northern approach. The railway terminus at Milsons Point is long gone, replaced first by the bridge construction workshop and then in 1935 by Luna Park. A symbol of post-Depression optimism, the amusement park is notable for the jaunty vernacular of its main buildings; Coney Island, Crystal Palace and the "face" entrance. Luna Park kept Sydneysiders amused until 1979, when a tragic fire in the Ghost Train ride closed the rundown park. Community affection ensured the survival of its buildings and their artwork, but the residents of the new apartment blocks nearby have not always been sympathetic. Restored and reopened during the 1990s, the Park was closed by complaints at a spectacular but noisy roller coaster. Luna Park is again open, with other events added to its traditional attractions.

Sydney Cove was known to the Aborigines as *warrang*. It has been the gateway to the city since European settlement in 1788. The sandstone wall of Semi-Circular Quay was built around the cove from the 1830s to the 1870s, making it narrower than the original shoreline. The qualifying adjective has since disappeared, leaving the puzzling title of Circular Quay, which has also overtaken the cove's picturesque earlier names.

In 1890, Circular Quay was dominated by ferry, rather than cargo, wharves—used by five million passengers a year. Ferry travel gained its peak patronage in the years shortly before the opening of the Harbour Bridge. In 1927 a total of 47 million trips were made. Ferries carry about a quarter of that total today, yet ferry commuting remains a quintessentially Sydney experience.

Circular Quay's role as a commuter interchange was enlarged in 1956, with the opening of its elevated railway station. Circular Quay Station completed the city rail loop which was planned decades earlier by J.J.C. Bradfield. The Cahill Expressway, built above the railway to take Harbour Bridge car traffic to the eastern suburbs, was not part of Bradfield's original plan. Bradfield and others had produced elegant architectural visions for a harbourside station; the expressway and 1950s' functionalism overpowered such delicacies. For the past 50 years the resulting structure has been condemned as an aesthetic disaster, dividing the city from its harbour. During the 1990s, the Australian Government even offered to fund an underground relocation of the Circular Quay railway; the expressway had recently been made partly redundant by the construction of a vehicular tunnel beneath the harbour.

Thomas Mort built his woolstore at Circular Quay in 1869 and extended it in 1887. When Mort established specialised wool sales on this site during the 1840s, local trading was disorganised and frequently dishonest. Mort's establishment of local auctions, broking and stores was important in making wool Australia's leading export during the 1800s, financing the growth of the colony and its capital. With its prime position on the edge of the Quay, Mort's business was eventually handling at least half of all the wool sold in Sydney. A decade after Thomas Mort's death in 1878, his firm merged with that of his Melbourne rival Richard Goldsbrough. Goldsbrough Mort transferred its wool handling operations to a new Darling Harbour store at Pyrmont. The water police court and police station were built across the road during the 1850s and now form the Justice and Police Museum.

The Goldsbrough Mort woolstore was demolished in 1960 to make way for Sydney's first skyscraper. From 1912 city building heights were limited to 45 metres (150 feet). The scrapping of this limit in 1957 unleashed an explosion of office tower construction. It also overlaid Sydney's sandstone and brick architecture with a new layer of glass, steel and concrete. Built for the insurance company AMP, the new building quickly became a well-liked feature of Sydney, partly because it occupied only half of its site, permitting a generous public space facing Circular Quay. Such liberality has not been typical of Sydney office towers. The City has permitted some of the largest floor-space-to-site ratios in the world, similar to those of Hong Kong. The result is a frequently untidy city streetscape of office towers dominating their site and neighbouring buildings and streets.

Sydney's first Customs House was built in 1845 on Sydney Cove's reclaimed mud flats, formalising the Cove's status as the official place of entry and departure for trade and immigration. Colonial Architect Mortimer Lewis designed a Greek Revival Customs House on this site. The purpose of the Customs House was to collect revenue (import duties and wharfage and tonnage rates) from the increased trade and passenger shipping that was frequenting the harbour. The first Customs House became too small for its purpose, and was replaced in 1887 by a larger building designed by Colonial Architect James Barnet in the style of an Italian palazzo. Two additional stories and a second ionic colonnade were added in 1903 by Barnet's successor, Walter Liberty Vernon.

As the Quay's role shifted from mercantile to commuter traffic in the twentieth century, the role of the Customs House diminished. However, the building continued to be used by the Customs Department until 1990, when it was remodeled as a multi-function site, with a focus on public access and increased civic space. Customs House has recently undergone another contemporary transformation into the Sydney City Library and offices. It also provides ample function space as well as a restaurant on the top level with expansive views of Sydney harbour. Loftus Street, to the right of the photo, is a major route for buses into Circular Quay. Although Sydney's buses follow most of the old tram routes, they have never replaced the trams in efficiency or affection. A new tram-line has opened, running from Central Station past Darling Harbour to inner western suburbs. However, proposals to extend this line through the city to Circular Quay are difficult to resolve and much debated.

ALFRED STREET, CIRCULAR QUAY

The passenger transport system of the city of Sydney was long dependent on trams. A demand had been created for this convenient and cheap mode of transport which could be met by no other means. Motor buses and motor cabs, however satisfactory they may have been in London or elsewhere, could never cope with the passenger traffic of Sydney. The photo shows the wide expanse which then linked the ferry wharves of Circular Quay to the City.

Electric trams outnumber horse-drawn vehicles; motor cars were not yet in sight. Sydney's first tram route ran from Circular Quay in 1861. Electric trams were introduced in 1899, superseding horse and steam trams. By the 1920s Sydney had one of the world's most extensive tramway systems, carrying over 300 million passengers each year.

Alfred Street continues its role as a transport terminus, although the trams have been replaced by buses, which battle through increasingly slow city traffic. In the first half of the twentieth century, trams helped maintain the city's pedestrian character, despite competition from buses and cars. However, the popularity of private cars after 1945 increased congestion of city streets and expanded the suburbs far beyond pre-War limits, and led to the abolition of the tram system. Sydney's last tram ran in 1961. Today, Circular Quay is a tourist promenade as well as a commuter interchange. This new function inspired further refurbishment for the 1988 Bicentenary and the Sydney Olympics. New granite footpaths, tree plantings, a new bus interchange and new ferry terminals were all part of the renovation of the city's gateways for the Sydney Olympics and the twenty-first century.

Wool and bond stores dominated the eastern side of Sydney Cove from the 1850s. They were built to service the wool trade, which had its wharves on the eastern side of the quay. The cargo trade occupied the western side. Circular Quay's wharves handled foreign trade until the 1870s, when the need for longer wharves for larger ships sent wharf owners and ships to Walsh Bay and Darling Harbour. The ferry commuter trade also competed for space at the Quay. New wharves elsewhere moved the maritime focus from Circular Quay, permitting the survival of most of the early warehouses deep into the twentieth century. Even in this 1892 photograph, the Quay is sleepy apart from the ferry wharves at the southern end of the Cove; taxicabs await ferry passengers nearby.

During the 1950s and 1960s the woolstores on East Circular Quay were demolished for Sydney's first high-rise office precinct—Bennelong House, Lend Lease House, ICI Building and Unilever House. The offices had a short life, replaced in 1999 by a new East Circular Quay development. Converting the quayside roadway into a pedestrian concourse, the new precinct offers more public access. The new buildings courted controversy, partly because of their close proximity to the Opera House and also because most of them are luxury apartments, and the privatisation of such a cherished area was widely disapproved (except by those sufficiently wealthy to become residents). However, the success of the spaces at ground level has won over public opinion. Day and night, the colonnade becomes a lively pedestrian area with tourists and Sydneysiders mingling at cafés and enjoying the view.

This view of the western shore of Sydney Cove includes some of the first substantial buildings constructed in Australia. The square, sandstone warehouses began life as the Commissariat Stores, built to house food, clothing, fuel and other essentials for the new colony's soldiers and convicts. The Stores were built by convicts around 1810, to a design by Colonel Foveaux of the New South Wales Corps. Part of the Stores complex is Cadman's Cottage, the oldest surviving residential building in Sydney. It was built in 1816 for the Governor's coxswain, John Cadman and his family. The area behind the western shore of Sydney Cove has been known as "The Rocks" since Sydney's first years of European occupation. The title reflects its steep, rocky terrain, its early sandstone quarries, and the raw character of its early convict housing and streets.

The Commissariat Stores were demolished in the 1930s to make way for the offices of the Maritime Service Board, which administered the harbour and wharves. The construction of the building was protracted due to Australia's involvement in World War II and was not completed until 1952. The building now houses the Museum of Contemporary Art, opened in 1991. The other large, new structure in the photograph is the Overseas Passenger Terminal, opened in 1960 and subsequently refurbished and used today mainly by holiday cruise ships. During the 1960s, the government of New South Wales planned to demolish most of the buildings in the Rocks and redevelop the entire area with apartment and office towers. Heritage campaigners and financial shortfalls eventually saved the Rocks for a more history-friendly development. The area is today the hub of Sydney tourism.

The small bay is Campbell's Cove, named for Robert Campbell, a Scottish merchant who built Sydney's first private trading wharf in 1801. Campbell's Wharf stretches from the right of Campbell's Cove, along the western side of Sydney Cove. The wharf was initially used by whalers, until the smell of boiling blubber brought complaints and the whalers' removal to more remote parts of the harbour. To the left of Campbell's Cove is Dawes Point, where a small fort was built from 1791. Intended to protect the colony from France, during the Napoleonic Wars, the battery was later considered security from the Russians during the Crimean War of the 1850s. The Fort was removed in the 1920s to make way for the Harbour Bridge. Dawes Point in 1901 featured a jumble of iron sheds and dinghies for hire. A year earlier the area was resumed by the government for reconstruction after the outbreak of bubonic plague.

Constructed from the 1820s, Robert Campbell's stores to the South of his cove are the only stores surviving from Sydney Cove's early trading days. They are now used as harbourside restaurants and shops. Another set of stores and Sydney's first domestic power station were built behind them in 1912, while in the century between these views, Campbell's Cove finger wharf was built and demolished. Towards the centre of the harbour in both views is Fort Denison, another fortress constructed on Pinchgut Island around 1855. Campbell's Cove is now encircled by the Park Hyatt, one of Sydney's leading hotels. Completed in 1989, the Hyatt's integration with the shoreline, nearby heritage buildings and public spaces, won civic design awards for its architect Ken Woolley. The Sydney Opera House opposite completes a celebrated urban tableau.

Fort Macquarie was built in 1817 on the tip of Bennelong Point, the southern side of Sydney Cove. The Point is named after Bennelong, an Aborigine kidnapped by Governor Phillip in 1789 to become a mediator between Sydney's established residents and its new arrivals. Phillip built a hut for Bennelong on the point, and he was briefly a prominent citizen of early Sydney, before travelling to London with Phillip in 1792. After his return a few years later, Bennelong's adoption of European dress and manners estranged him from his people. Fort Macquarie mounted 15 guns against would-be invaders. The Fort was designed by Francis Greenway, a convict and Australia's first architect. Transported for forgery in 1814, he quickly became a favourite of Governor Macquarie, designing most of early Sydney's public buildings. This photo was taken shortly before its demolition in 1901.

Occupied by a tram-shed until the 1950s, Bennelong Point is now the site of Australia's most famous building. In 1957 an international design competition for a Sydney opera house was won by Jørn Utzon, a Danish architect. Despite Utzon's relative obscurity, the brilliance of his proposal made the Opera House famous even before construction began. Dissolving the normal language of walls and roof, Utzon placed most of the building within a massive granite podium contiguous to the harbour, while the theatres occupy distinct shell-like structures above. The foyers are placed at the harbour end, and the podium became the entry point. But Utzon's vision for the interior was never realised. He was forced to leave the project in 1966, well before the building's completion in 1973. His dismissal sparked a long-running controversy—though in 1999 he was re-engaged to outline design principles for the building's future, and then in 2002 as principal architect for new building projects.

Known as Woccanmagully by the local Aboriginal inhabitants, the Cadigal, Farm Cove gained its current name from the siting of the first government farm; nine acres of corn and barley planted by the cove in 1788. This first antipodean attempt at European agriculture proved a failure, and the infant colony teetered on the brink of starvation for a few years. After successful farms were founded elsewhere, the shores of Farm Cove were leased out for private farming before being absorbed within the "Governor's Domain" and the Botanic Gardens. The Governor's Domain was set aside in 1788 by Governor Phillip as his private reserve. The Botanic Gardens were established on this site in 1816 by Governor Macquarie with the opening of the road to "Mrs Macquarie's Chair". Carved out of rock as a spectacular vantage point for the harbour, it remains a popular destination to this day.

The Gardens have continued to expand, occupying most of the space by Farm Cove originally allotted to the Governor's Domain. Descendants of the area's original swamp oaks and red gums cohabit with plantings from throughout Sydney and Australia. The botanical display is set off by statuary, mostly imported from Italy during the 1870s and 1880s, although the work of local sculptors is also represented. Recent years have seen a revival of the practice of commissioning artists to create works for the Gardens. The City skyline, once dominated by the Colonial Secretary's Office and Government House, is now a showplace for corporate architecture. Phillip Street Tower, Chifley Tower, Aurora Place and Governor Phillip Tower, contending statements by Sir Norman Foster, Renzo Piano and other notable architects, step down the Macquarie Street ridge.

In July 1817 Governor Lachlan Macquarie commissioned architect Francis Greenway to prepare plans for a new government house and stables. The stables were to be part of the picturesque landscape surrounding the proposed Government House and consisted of horse stalls, boxes and staff quarters arranged around a central courtyard. Finally completed in 1821, they were the most elaborate stables in New South Wales. During the nineteenth century alterations were made to the building to house additional staff and in the early 1900s a motor garage was added. In 1912 an Advisory Committee for an Academy of Fine Arts recommended that a Conservatorium of Music be established. The stables were chosen as the site, with existing rooms converted to offices and an auditorium constructed in the central courtyard. The Conservatorium opened in 1916, under the direction of Henri Verbrugghen.

In May 1997 the Premier of New South Wales, the Honorable Bob Carr MP announced a major upgrade of the Conservatorium with the goal of creating a world class music education facility. The project was a complex collaboration between the Department of Education and Training and the Department of Public Works and Services, the architects, acoustic consultants, the key users, and the Principal of the Conservatorium High School, the Royal Botanic Gardens, the Domain Trust and many others. Heritage considerations were important and sensitive. The redevelopment has restored Greenway's historic castellated building, removing newer additions to the structure while increasing the area of the school by enhancing and enlarging the public green space of the Royal Botanic Gardens. For the Conservatorium, it has created facilities of outstanding acoustic and architectural quality.

The first Government House was built on Bridge Street in 1788. Replacement of this rudimentary structure quickly became a priority of early colonial Governors. In 1816 Governor Lachlan Macquarie commissioned Francis Greenway to design a new grand residence and stables in the castellated style. However, Macquarie was considered extravagant by the British Government and only the stables were built. After decades of protest, the construction of a new vice-regal residence was authorised in 1835. Governor Sir Richard Bourke requested that "some eminent architect in London" be commissioned and Edward Blore, special architect to King William IV, was selected but never visited the colony. Delayed by economic depression, the building was finally completed in 1845, the most sophisticated example of Gothic Revival architecture in the colony.

Today, the site is a grand ensemble of buildings, gardens and contents, retaining much of its nineteenth-century character, however, developments over 150 years provide evidence of changing tastes and social attitudes. The exterior of the house has had few alterations and the ground floor State Rooms contain an outstanding collection of nineteenth- and twentieth-century furnishings and decoration. These were commissioned from leading Sydney craftsmen and artists and reflect changing fashion and differing tastes of the governors and their wives. The house is now managed by the Historic Houses Trust and is open to the public, and while no longer the residence of the Governor, it continues to be used for vice-regal ceremonies and State occasions. The best of contemporary and decorative arts have been commissioned for the refurbishment of the State Rooms.

In keeping with the early nineteenth-century fashion for "picturesque" settings, Government House was sited high on a harbour headland overlooking the water. The gardens immediately around the house began to be laid out during its construction in the 1840s. In the early 1860s this area of the garden, the Eastern Terrace, was created and it marked the change in horticultural fashion from the picturesque to a more formal, Italianate style.

This terrace was the grandest garden feature in New South Wales, with sandstone walls topped with urns, and gravel paths set out around a central pond, a fountain and ornamental garden beds. The central axial pathway focussed the view down the harbour with wider views of the water from the terrace. The Eastern Terrace became the showpiece of the garden and the focus for entertainment outdoors.

Unlike most other surviving colonial houses in Sydney, Government House has retained its setting and, most importantly, its relationship with the harbour. Much of the nineteenth-century character of the grounds remains and the overall form of the Eastern Terrace survives, with its sandstone walls, pathways and original fountain. The central pathway continues to act as the focus, leading to an uninterrupted view over the harbour to Sydney Heads.

The main axial view is framed by two *Araucaria columnaris* (Cook Island Pines), planted circa 1870 and part of the important collection of historic trees in the grounds. While the form of the early ornamental garden beds of the Eastern Terrace has been lost, the current planting is representative of nineteenth century garden species. The Eastern Terrace is the focus for entertainment of guests following State receptions and similar functions.

The photo shows the central transept of the Garden Palace, built in the Botanic Gardens for the 1879 Sydney International Exhibition. After London's Great Exhibition of the 1850s, cities competed to display the quality and extent of their industrial and primary products, as well as artworks and other achievements.

The design and construction of the Garden Palace was completed in slightly more than eighteen months, a remarkable achievement given its size (31,000 square metres of floor space) and elaborate decoration. The interior was adorned with frescoes and statuary, including this one of Queen Victoria, while the exterior was an extravaganza of domes and turrets. Over one million people visited the Garden Palace during the seven months of the Exhibition.

The Garden Palace fell victim to its speedy construction. Lacking a local iron industry, Colonial Architect James Barnet was forced to use timber, sheet iron and glass for the structure. In 1882 the Palace was destroyed in a spectacular fire.

The Garden Palace was widely mourned, yet its destruction at least added its substantial site to the Botanic Gardens. During the 1880s the site was reborn as the Palace Gardens, entered by elaborate gates sculpted as a memorial to the Palace. The main feature of this part of the Garden is the Governor Phillip memorial fountain. Commissioned in 1888, the monument was not completed until 1897, delayed in part by political and aesthetic debates. Its sculptor, Achille Simonetti, pressured by advocates of allegorical and naturalistic sculpture, produced an ungainly combination of the two: a portrait statue of Phillip surmounts four classical allegories of Commerce, Agriculture, Mining and Navigation. Opposite the gardens is the State Library, built in stages from 1905. Its Greek portico was not added until the 1930s.

Bridge Street gains its name from the wooden bridge which crossed the Tank Stream near Macquarie Place. This freshwater stream emptied into Sydney Cove, inspiring the choice of the Cove as the site of the first settlement. Now encased in drains, the Tank Stream still flows beneath the city from near Hyde Park to Sydney Cove. By 1900, Bridge Street was Sydney's most impressive thoroughfare, dominated by the domes of the Colonial Secretary's Office and the Lands Building. It was also the site of the first Government House and now the location for the Museum of Sydney. Together with the General Post Office and Martin Place, Bridge Street embodied Sir Henry Parkes' ambition to shape Sydney as an urban monument to progress and democratic government.

The eastern end of Bridge Street remains a government precinct, but its western end, nearest the camera, retains the commercial focus established by the Royal Exchange building on the Pitt Street corner. The centre of the Sydney wool trade from its construction in 1851 and home of the Sydney Stock Exchange from 1872, the Exchange building was replaced by an office tower during the 1960s. Another commercial landmark still stands, the Burns Philp offices, built for a firm of South Sea traders around 1900. Beyond this Romanesque structure is Liner House, a small office building completed in 1960. This Modernist landmark features interior sculpture and décor by Douglas Annand, a leading Sydney sculptor of the 1950s and 1960s. Sydney Stock Exchange has recently returned to Bridge Street opposite Liner House.

Completed in 1880, the Colonial Secretary's Office was the first of the government offices designed by James Barnet. Despite their prosaic purpose, this series of grand sandstone palaces redefined the look and many of the spaces of colonial Sydney. The Colonial Secretary's Office and the Lands Building formed an imposing dress circle above Circular Quay. Barnet took advantage of the 1879 International Exhibition's boost of Sydney's artistic community. Among the sculptors exhibiting at the Exhibition were the Italians Achille Simonetti and Giovanni Fontana, who gained commissions for the Colonial Secretary's Office. The corner niches house allegorical figures by Simonetti; those visible in this photo embody Wisdom, Justice and Mercy. Fontana adorned the interior with portrait statues of Queen Victoria and her son Prince Albert, plus a striking allegorical figure of New South Wales.

The Colonial Secretary headed the main bureaucracy of colonial New South Wales, its regulatory and licensing responsibilities later taken by other departments and the state Premier. Notably, Sir Henry Parkes, the colony's most influential politician, occupied both roles. The building features a lavish office frequently used by Parkes, who often resided in the building. Such was the demand for space in the building that the new Colonial Architect, Walter Liberty Vernon, added an extra floor of offices and dome in 1896. Barnet was displeased, dubbing his successor "Vernon the vandal". With the decline of the Chief Secretary's role other government bureaucrats, as well as industrial courts and tribunals have occupied the Office. However, the building has thus far escaped the fate of the Treasury Office across the road, now the portico and foyer to an international hotel.

The Lands Department Building was designed by James Barnet and built between 1876 and 1894. Occupying a whole block between Bridge and Bent Streets, the building surrounds a central court and is the largest of Barnet's several city buildings, dominating the Circular Quay precinct. Designed in 'Italian Renaissance of the Venetian type', the visual rhythm of windows, arcades and loggia is typical of Barnet's work, breaking an otherwise ponderous composition and creating a verandah-like connection with the building's setting opposite Macquarie Place. The building incorporated emerging technologies of heating, lighting and a communication system which operated through speaking tubes and pneumatic bells. The copper dome and lantern above the Bridge Street façade was initially intended to house an observatory.

During the 1890s, statues were installed in 23 of the Lands Buildings' 48 niches. Sculpted by several artists, the portrait statues of explorers, botanists and politicians associated with land policy were a self-conscious attempt to give sanction to the often shady business of land exploration, sale and resale. The Lands Department was established in 1856 to administer the mapping, sale, usage and lease of land in New South Wales. The size of the Lands Office may seem excessive for such a prosaic purpose; however, land sale and speculation has been a major Australian industry since the beginning of European settlement. With home ownership now widely dispersed in Australia, property speculation has become a democratic pastime.

Wynyard Square was initially a barrack square for the George Street Military Barracks. It became a public park in 1855. Small in size, Wynyard Square's character has changed with that of the surrounding buildings. At Federation, Wynyard was a fashionable part of town, and the park resembled those of London's West End, surrounded by tall residences and retailers specialising in expensive furniture and fashion. Overseas consulates were attracted to the area, and Petty's Hotel, nearby on York Street, became the preferred hotel for many of Sydney's most distinguished visitors. Giovanni Fontana's statue of John Dunmore Lang—Presbyterian Minister, republican and politician—focuses the southern end of the Square. Unveiled in 1891, the statue was primarily financed by public subscriptions, underlining the elite tone of the precinct.

Wynyard Square began to lose its exclusivity during the 1920s, with the conversion of several Victorian residences to boarding houses. During the 1920s, the park and York Street were excavated for the construction of Wynyard underground station, connecting the City Railway to the Harbour Bridge. Above the station on York Street was built Railway House, an Art Deco office building distinctive for its green glazed terracotta cladding. The radio tower of the AWA Building seen in the distant right was the city's tallest structure when constructed in 1939. The new influx of commuters and office workers boosted the clientele of the hotels on both sides of the Square, but this combination also gave the Square a slightly seedy reputation. However, the Menzies Hotel was one of several 1960s improvements to the precinct, returning some of Wynyard's former glamour.

In 1882 Hunter Street boasted a "heterogeneous collection of stationery, books, music, jewellery, French goods, taxidermists and sewing machine repositories", while the continuation up the hill to Macquarie Street, was apportioned to offices, hotels and private residences. The young Henry Parkes set up business in Hunter Street, and lived—as did many shopkeepers—above the shop. His shop and residence were in the building occupied in this photograph by E. Cantor, Shirtmaker, and McCarthy's Pharmacy. Established in 1845, Parkes' "fancy-ware depot" sold children's toys, carved ivory pieces and imported goods. Four years after setting up business, Parkes made his first public speech, and launched his political career.

The shops and hotels of Victorian Hunter Street are no more. The city from Bridge Street to Martin Place is the commercial centre of Sydney with city "suits" filling the streets during the day. The 1880s photo includes the Royal Mail Hotel facing the Currency Lass Hotel from opposite corners of Pitt, O'Connell and Hunter, but their places were subsequently taken by the offices of banks and insurers. Also occupying this corner was the prominent cornice of the *Sydney Morning Herald* offices, a magnet for job seekers and penurious readers since the 1870s. During the 1920s the *Herald* expanded into the grander domed building which still dominates the Pitt Street corner. Eventually occupied by a bank, the Herald building is now home to the Radisson Plaza Hotel.

Brought into being by the construction of the General Post Office (GPO), Martin Place started out as a narrow laneway between Pitt and George Streets. Built from 1866, the GPO was planned by James Barnet as a new centrepiece for Sydney, both in communications and urban space. Like Barnet's other city projects, the GPO was orientated north towards the harbour, creating the expectation of a public space to frame and enhance the new structure. However, the laneway survived until the completion of the GPO to Pitt Street in 1891. The buildings opposite were demolished and it could finally be appreciated. Even then, the vast piazza envisaged by Barnet was reduced to a 30-metre (100-foot) wide street. Financially stretched by the 1890s Depression, the government sold off the remainder of the new space.

The 1908–9 Royal Commission on The Improvement of Sydney and its Suburbs recommended the extension of Martin Place up to Macquarie Street, arguing that this final extension would "bring the official street into closer touch with the centre of the city". In 1935 the entire street was opened up to Macquarie Street. The significance of Martin Place had already been heightened in 1929 with the unveiling of the Cenotaph sculpted by Bertram Mackennal. The simplicity of this memorial—a plain granite block guarded by two bronzes of contemporary servicemen—attracted intense criticism. It has since become a well-loved monument, site of the annual Anzac Day dawn service. In 1969 Martin Place was finally converted into a pedestrian plaza, achieving something of Barnet's original vision. The broad avenue remains Sydney's principal civic space.

Designed to rival its European counterparts in architectural grandeur, the GPO is Sydney's most lavishly-decorated building. Like the Colonial Secretary's Office in Bridge Street, the GPO gained an extra floor of offices shortly after its completion, compromising the clean cornice line of the original structure. The GPO represents a spectacular period of innovation in communications. Cheap international postage was a novelty when the GPO building was begun. When completed, it embraced electric telegram and telephone communication, enhancing its status. More recent advances in electronic communications diminished the GPO's relevance. The clock tower of the GPO dominated the Sydney skyline for many years and remained the tallest Sydney structure until the AWA communications tower was built in 1939. The tower was dismantled during World War II.

The Commonwealth Bank occupies the Pitt Street corner opposite the GPO. Established by the Australian government as the first bank empowered to conduct both savings and trading business, the Commonwealth's head office in Martin Place established the precinct as the banking centre of Sydney and Australia. Generations of Australian children saved coins in money box replicas of this building. Completed in 1916, the Bank was one of several bank and insurance offices constructed near the GPO, lining Martin Place with complementary sandstone structures. Despite this, Martin Place has retained a varied character, lined during the 1930s by addresses as diverse as Sydney's first milk bar, the nightclubs Prince's and Romano's, the Hotel Australia and the first eatery of the Cahill's restaurant chain. Martin Place has become more populist in focus since its conversion to pedestrian use.

As well as providing a sheltered arcade from the sun, heat and rain, the colonnade on three sides of the GPO formed a civic connection between the building's interior and Martin Place, Pitt and George Streets. Its arches were decorated with allegorical heads representing the other colonies and nations with which post and telegraphic communications were conducted. These were among 51 sculpted keystone heads also representing classical gods, the seasons, explorers, politicians and royalty. The base of the clock tower features statues of Queen Victoria, Britannia and Australia. More controversially, the Pitt Street façade is decorated with relief sculptures of law, agriculture and other trades and professions. These realist representations of contemporary life caused a political storm during the 1880s. A parliamentary inquiry recommended that they be "cut out" from the building. Fortunately this recommendation was not enacted.

The base course, carved capitals and the polished columns of the GPO were built with native grey granite from Moruya on the south coast of New South Wales. The rest of the building is built with distinctive Sydney sandstone. In 2000 the GPO was converted to a hotel and retail centre. Although still offering postal services, the major part of the building is now occupied by a hotel with a new tower built behind the main building. Complete with marks left a century ago by "strike anywhere" phosphorus matches, the colonnade can still be enjoyed. It faces the lively pedestrian precinct of Martin Place—a lunchtime gathering place for city workers.

Macquarie Street is Sydney's most prestigious street, running from the Opera House to Hyde Park. The street was established by its namesake, Lachlan Macquarie, who, on arrival in Sydney in 1810, planned a new hospital and road next to the Domain. Nicknamed the Rum Hospital, because a monopoly of rum importation was the payment granted the contractors who constructed it, the new hospital's three buildings and their verandahs extended for much of Macquarie Street's length. By the 1850s, two of the hospital buildings had been adapted as Parliament House and the Mint building. The central building was replaced in 1894 by a new Sydney Hospital building. The "Iron Church", St. Stephen's Presbyterian, stood on Macquarie Street for over 40 years. It was prefabricated in Glasgow and erected next to Parliament House in 1857.

The space once occupied by the Iron Church now hosts the most recent extension to the State Library of NSW. The Library is known to many Sydneysiders as "the Mitchell", in recognition of David Scott Mitchell whose vast collection of Australiana was bequeathed to New South Wales on the condition that a library be built for it. A work in progress for much of the past century, the State Library now matches the ambitions of its first benefactor.

Facing the Domain and Botanic Gardens, Macquarie Street was by the 1850s the city's most desirable residential street. After 1900 it became the site of the city's first apartment blocks, some also providing chambers to medical and legal practitioners. Both of these characters have persisted—"Macquarie Street specialist" is shorthand for expensive attention, while the Astor remains among Sydney's most exclusive apartment addresses.

In 1810 Governor Lachlan Macquarie formalised the setout and naming of the streets of Sydney. The eastern boundary of the town was marked by the creation of Macquarie Street and at its southern end, the area known as the Racecourse was renamed and formally defined, becoming Hyde Park. It was here, at the southern end of Macquarie Street, that the governor sited the colony's most ambitious public buildings. The three-wing General Hospital was constructed between 1811 and 1816 and this was followed by the convict Barracks, St. James Church and the Supreme Court House. The hospital was converted for both Parliament and the Royal Mint, while the Hyde Park Barracks was used as law courts and by government departments from 1830. The precinct was increasingly seen as the seat of government and the law, its central space named Chancery Square, dominated by a statue of Queen Victoria.

Renamed Queens Square, the area remains a focus of government and law, continuing its role as the most important civic precinct of Sydney. To mark the Bicentennial of European settlement in Australia, the Square underwent a major refurbishment in 1988. The former hospital wing (obscured by trees on the left) was used as law courts after the Royal Mint closed in 1926, and then became a museum in 1982. A conservation and redevelopment project for the former Mint buildings, to create the head office of the Historic Houses Trust of New South Wales, was completed in 2004. The Hyde Park Barracks (on the right) was also converted to museum use in the early 1980s. Saved in response to mounting public concern for its significance, it was restored to its convict era of occupation. It now has a focus on its own history and the many occupants it housed over 180 years.

Originally named Chancery Square, the space at the head of King Street was renamed Queens Square in 1881 by the premier Henry Parkes. However, the Queen Victoria statue intended for the square was destroyed in the Garden Palace fire. Commissioning of a replacement statue sparked fierce debate in Sydney artistic and political circles. The embryonic republican movement demanded that Australian subjects be celebrated, and joined local sculptors in protesting the choice of J.E. Boehm as sculptor. A friend and favourite artist of Queen Victoria, Boehm's work created further disagreement on its unveiling in 1888. Behind the statue is St. James Church, designed by Francis Greenway. The eastern porch facing the square was added during the 1830s by John Verge. With Greenway's 1819 convict Barracks on the opposite side of the Square and the Law Courts behind it, St. James is the centrepiece of a fine Georgian ensemble.

Most of Queens Square was closed to traffic during the 1980s, and the Queen Victoria statue was relocated as part of the new pedestrian precinct. Francis Greenway's ability to exploit the simple materials available to the early colony is evident in St. James' austere elegance. It was intended to be a school, part of a civic square of courts and other government buildings. The 1970s Supreme Court building at the right, although overshadowing the other colonial buildings in the precinct, has restored that intention. Its location also continues the legal flavour of the precinct, established when the first Supreme Court was built in the 1820s. Although courts of various jurisdictions sit in other parts of the city, lawyers' chambers remain concentrated in the St. James area and Macquarie Street, where they cohabit with those of medical specialists. Dominating the view is the Centrepoint Tower, completed in 1981.

Named by Governor Macquarie for his wife, Elizabeth Campbell, Elizabeth Street was a fashionable residential street, with elegant terrace houses overlooking the maturing Hyde Park. Obscured by the trees on the left is the Supreme Court building. The towers of Sydney's Great Synagogue to the right were almost alone in exceeding domestic scale. Built between Elizabeth and Pitt Streets and completed in 1878, the Synagogue resulted from the merger of the two main Sydney Jewish congregations. Architecturally reminiscent of the City of London Great Synagogue, its scale, extravagant decoration and prominent location were powerful statements of the presence and status of Sydney's Jewish community. Beyond the Synagogue, the character of Elizabeth Street became somewhat less exclusive. By 1900, pubs and the odd private club—including Tattersall's bookmakers club—were a feature of the street. Past Hyde Park, Elizabeth Street met the factories, warehouses and boarding houses of Surry Hills.

The corner of Elizabeth and Market is often known as "David Jones corner" after the department store which opened there in 1927. Like most Sydney department stores, David Jones began business as one of the city's numerous drapers. During the 1880s, the store adopted the European trend towards retailing a range of goods under one roof. It also began manufacturing many of its own products at its own factory. Until the 1960s David Jones was one of several city department stores, competing with Anthony Horderns, Mark Foys, Farmers, Marcus Clark, McDowells, Grace Bros, Snows and others. Only Grace Bros (recently renamed Myer after its Melbourne parent company) has survived with David Jones, the others falling victim to the suburbanisation and increased specialisation of retailing. David Jones also prospered from its canny relocation opposite St. James Railway Station, and its cultivation of a "society" image. Upmarket retailers and hotels now dominate the next block, towering over the Synagogue.

King Street is one of the oldest Sydney streets. Named after Governor King, one of the colony's earliest governors, it has been a major east-west city route for almost two centuries. In Federation times the street comprised three distinct sections. At its western end King Street served the Darling Harbour wharves and warehouses; the middle section was crowded with retailers, newspapers, lawyers' chambers and numerous hotels. King Street's upper reach was dominated by the imposing buildings of Sydney's justice system. Like most city streets of the late 1800s, King Street gathered together a wide variety of people and activities: warehouses, men's mercers, tobacconists, hotels, confectioners, theatres, shoemakers, barristers and solicitors, auctioneers, druggists, silk merchants, fish and oyster merchants and bakers. Many people lived above shops and other businesses. King Street had a reputation for debauchery and drunkenness—hardly surprising given that it boasted 22 hotels in the immediate vicinity.

King Street remains a major retail and office precinct. However, its appearance has altered significantly in the past century. The north side is now dominated by two large office and retail towers, examples of the 1960s and 1970s consolidation of city blocks into "super blocks". NRMA House (formerly the American Express Building) and the MLC Centre project a radically different scale at pedestrian level to their Federation predecessors.

On King Street's south side, much of the architecture, if not the businesses and vocations, of the Federation era can still be seen today. These survivors include the Sydney Arcade façade, the Australian Mutual Fire Insurance Building—one of the first large office buildings constructed on King Street—and the much loved Darrell Lea shop, originally created for Ashdown & Co., wholesale and furnishing Ironmongers.

Theatre has been performed on the site of the Theatre Royal since 1832, when Barnett Levey's temporary theatre staged its first production. The second Theatre Royal opened in 1875, after its predecessor was destroyed by fire. The main entrance to the theatre was in Castlereagh Street, with the stalls entrance in King Street. The Royal was the centre of Sydney's commercial theatre district, with several theatres and auditoriums in the nearby streets. The pubs that surrounded the Theatre Royal are long gone. King Street had a reputation for debauchery and drunkenness which derived from the hotels and the theatre; its night life was a magnet for Sydneysiders.

The present Theatre Royal is the result of a public outcry after the third Theatre Royal was closed in 1972 to make way for the MLC Centre, a 65-storey office tower and shopping arcade designed by Harry Seidler. Building workers' unions, actors and heritage enthusiasts combined to demand the inclusion of a theatre in the new development. This campaign promoted the theatrical history of King Street. Signposted at street level, the new Theatre Royal occupies the King Street face of this imposing building, with the new theatre projecting a radically different scale at pedestrian level to its Federation predecessor. The above-ground pedestrian walkway built in the 1990s has impacted on the vista up King Street to the civic and justice precinct of Macquarie Street.

Running from Hyde Park to the wharves of Darling Harbour, Market Street is one of the main city thoroughfares. In 1811 Governor Macquarie ordered the produce markets at King Street Wharf be moved to a new market between George and York Street. The markets established Market Street as Sydney's main shopping street, crowded with vehicles transporting goods from the wharfs and lined with warehouses, shops and hotels. Saturday night, when the shops stayed open until ten o'clock, was the workers' gala night when young men and women gathered together and "did the block". In an era without motorcars, the densely-packed street was a lively scene with people jostling with hansom cabs, and trams trying to navigate a path through.

The opening in 1926 of St. James Railway Station at this Hyde Park end of Market Street cemented Market Street's popularity with shoppers. David Jones joined the major stores of Farmers (now Myer), Grace Bros (now also Myer) and Gowings on Market Street. From the 1920s, the area also offered numerous cinemas, although only the State survives from a long list including the Embassy, Liberty, Palace, Esquire and Lyceum. City cinema-going has declined since the 1960s as suburban multiplexes offered new competition. Pubs and retailers have proved more resilient. The brewers could afford the best corner sites, and many are still occupied by hotels and former hotel buildings. These include the Albion on the Elizabeth Street corner. Later rebuilt and renamed the St. James, this hotel building now houses a luxury fashion house.

The Queen Victoria Building was designed by city architect George McRae, who famously offered the City Council a choice of four architectural styles for the new market: Gothic, Queen Anne, Renaissance and Romanesque. Architectural debates of the 1800s were marked by a "battle of the styles" between the advocates of Gothic and the more secular Classical revivals. By the 1890s, these arguments had lost much of their intellectual coherence, and were further confused as Romanesque joined the contending revivals, as had the more contemporary Queen Anne. As City Architect, McRae produced buildings in a range of styles. The Council's choice of Romanesque was appropriate to the imposing scale of the new building, and provided suitably grand arched entrances to the main arcade. The QVB's domes have been a feature of the City's skyline since its completion in 1898.

Apart from the intrusive Monorail, this view from York Street remains elegantly closed by Sydney Town Hall. The QVB carried the stigma of failure until its triumphant 1980s revival. Among the many replacement proposals was one for a Council car park. Another would have swept away the QVB in favour of a widened York Street, speeding car traffic towards the Harbour Bridge. Despite its early disappointments, the QVB can now be appreciated as a brilliant example of the covered shopping street, worthy of comparison with contemporaries such as Milan's Galleria Vittorio Emmanuel and Naples's Galleria Umberto.

The Sydney Town Hall was built on the site of the old town cemetery between 1868 and 1889. A site on Bridge Street was originally chosen for the Town Hall, but the city council fought for land nearer the market places and trading precincts of the Darling Harbour area so that the city government would be located within the commercial centre of Sydney. The site selected, between St. Andrew's Cathedral and George Street markets, placed the Town Hall within a traditional civic relation to church and marketplace. However, this site necessitated the exhumation of the Old Sydney Burial Ground. The Town Hall was built in stages, the tower, offices and reception room facing George Street being completed by 1880 when Mayor Robert Fowler hosted the first event in the Vestibule. Despite its name, Centennial Hall was not completed until 1889, missing the 1888 centenary of European settlement.

During its 120-year history, Sydney Town Hall has retained the same function, still the centre of local government in Sydney and host to many functions, talks and concerts. This is rare in Sydney where many of the city's other historic buildings have been transformed to different uses as their functions have been re-defined. Originally lacking a civic square, the space between Sydney Town Hall and St. Andrew's was converted into Sydney Square in the 1970s. The Town Hall's expansive steps replaced the entry portico in 1934, when tunneling for the underground railway destabilised the area, and the substantial gate piers and iron palisade fencing were removed to St. Joseph's College in Hunters Hill. The front steps have become a favourite meeting place for Sydneysiders ever since. The clock tower, once a significant landmark in Sydney, is now dwarfed by the skyscrapers in the vicinity.

In Victorian Sydney, retail, residential and industrial worlds collided. Bathurst Street was no exception with its combination of housing, clothing shops, pawnbrokers, bookshops, warehouses and sheltered footpath spaces. In the early twentieth century this changed as housing and industry migrated to the suburbs. The obelisk at the Hyde Park end of Bathurst Street, erected in 1857 by Mayor George Thornton, is a sewer ventilation stack built when Sydney was often described as "smelling like a drain". The problems of water supply and waste disposal were tackled more systematically and successfully during the Federation decades. Despite its handsome Egyptian style, the obelisk was nicknamed the "Hyde Park Scent Bottle". It is essentially a replica of an Egyptian monument—Cleopatra's Needle—transported to London and re-erected there in the 1870s.

The blue Monorail compromises the Bathurst Street vista. Constructed in 1987, the Monorail is a controversial attempt to link the city to the Darling Harbour shopping and entertainment precinct. It has struggled for patronage, although its elevated views have made it a favourite with tourists. The Horizon apartment tower in the distance was designed by Harry Seidler and built in 1998. Bathurst Street is now framed by office buildings and some of the new apartment buildings which have produced a growth in the resident population in the city of Sydney. Hemmed in between Darling Harbour, Hyde Park and the Domain, the city's small area made city property prohibitively expensive for all but office and retail investors. During the past two decades city living has returned to favour, sparking a boom in construction of apartment towers and related social infrastructure.

Dedicated as a public recreation ground and military exercise field by Governor Macquarie in 1810, the park was used the same year for Sydney's first race meeting. It continued this role until 1821 and as a cricket ground until 1856. The central avenue was established and planted by 1860, though the other pathways were not shaded until the 1880s. The statue visible at the Macquarie Street end of the avenue was unveiled in 1866, commemorating Prince Albert. Fortunately, a railway terminus, proposed in the 1880s for the north-western corner of Hyde Park—which involved the demolition of St. James and the Supreme Court—never eventuated. However, Hyde Park was excavated during the 1920s for the construction of the City Railway and Museum and St. James stations. At this time Prince Albert's statue was removed to a site near the Conservatorium of Music.

Work on the City Railway alienated the public from the Park from 1918 to the end of the 1920s. A competition for the remodelling of the park was held in 1926 and won by Norman Weekes. Following the completion of the underground railway, Hyde Park was regenerated and replanted to its current design by Weekes, with the addition of two Art Deco monuments. At the northern end of the Park, the central fig tree avenue meets the Archibald Fountain, designed to commemorate the alliance between Australia and France during World War I. The fountain is named for its benefactor, J.F. Archibald, publisher and Francophile. The creation of the French sculptor François Sicard, the Archibald has become Sydney's favourite ornamental fountain. Surmounted by a bronze Apollo, it also includes statues of Diana the Huntress, Theseus and the Minotaur, and Jason and the Golden Fleece.

In the early years of the colony, all the churches built were Anglican, and Irish convicts were denied the right to worship according to the Catholic faith. After the arrival of two Catholic chaplains in 1820, a fund was launched to build a Catholic church. Land was granted for construction in the eastern part of town. Its position was cause for debate among Catholics, as the eastern end of town was not then as fashionable as the western side. The first St. Mary's was burnt down in 1865 and architect William Wardell engaged to design a replacement. Wardell had proved his Gothic credentials with Melbourne's Catholic cathedral. Given the expense of the project, St. Mary's Cathedral was built in stages, as funds became available from 1865 to 1899. The location, commanding the ridge between the Domain and Hyde Park, has given St. Mary's Cathedral a prominence denied St. Andrew's.

Built in yellow block sandstone from nearby Pyrmont, the Cathedral remains the spiritual home for Sydney Catholics. Thirty steps were added at the front of the church after Wardell's death, because an apparent error in the starting point of the building placed its entry in the middle of Cathedral Street. After lengthy negotiations, the City Council altered the street pattern in front of the Cathedral. The spires were part of the original design but have only recently been completed. Sydney's former Catholic Archbishop, Cardinal Clancy, launched a public appeal in 1995 in order to raise $27 million for the Cathedral's preservation and construction of the spires. Also recently restored is the Fraser Fountain at the rear. The fountain was not merely decorative; the city's water supply was unreliable and only the wealthy could rely on piped water.

Hyde Park originally comprised roughly 22 hectares (56 acres), including Elizabeth and most of College Streets, one third larger than it is today. It was divided by the extension of Park Street in the 1830s, however, subsequently Macquarie Street was closed through the park and became a pedestrian thoroughfare, often described as "Lovers Walk". From 1856 the Hyde Park Improvement Committee began improvements. Well-kept gravel walks intersected the park and it was beautified by numerous gardens of ornamental plants. The central avenue was lined with Moreton Bay Figs running the length of the park and substantial seats were placed in sheltered locations or ones with a view. Parts of the park were lost to road widening in the early 1900s and then it was severely impacted on by the construction of the City Railway in the 1920s. It was at this time that "Lovers Walk" disappeared.

The southern half of Hyde Park is dominated by the Anzac Memorial, designed by Bruce Dellit, a young architect barely out of college when he won the contest to design it, in 1929. The structure, made of grey-pink Bathurst granite, is one of Sydney's most symbolic buildings. Dellit's handling of decoration and form brings great solemnity to the Memorial. The cast-stone sculptures and bronze relief panels decorating the façades depict events and personnel involved in World War I and were executed by Rayner Hoff, the leading sculptor of the period. Ceremonial stairs take visitors inside to view the central sculpture group, Sacrifice, in the Hall of Silence, illuminated by amber glazed windows. While the Archibald Fountain at the northern end of Hyde Park and the Anzac Memorial commemorate different aspects of the War, they form a powerful pair located in the central green space of the city.

The Australian Museum was established in 1827, inspired by the need to collect and study Australia's "rare and curious" fauna and flora. The early collection and study of zoology and minerals was later augmented by anthropological and historical collections. The Museum is Australia's first public museum and the work of successive Government Architects, commencing with the Long Gallery designed by Mortimer Lewis during the 1840s, and still in use. This wing can be partly seen behind the grand College Street wing and portico, opened in 1868. Its architect, James Barnet, had plans for a grander composition extending down William Street, accommodating a public library and art gallery as well as the natural history museum. Despite being incomplete, Barnet's museum was one of Sydney's largest buildings, setting a new standard for public architecture in the colony.

The Museum today presents something of a blank face to William Street, partly in response to its crowding in by the street's widening into a major traffic thoroughfare. The William Street extension, the Parkes-Farmer Wing, was completed in 1963, adding offices and scientists' workspaces rather than extra galleries. The 1910 southern wing designed by Walter Liberty Vernon had already much expanded the Museum's display space. The Australian Museum has lagged behind the Sydney museum boom which has seen major extensions to the Art Gallery and the State Library, the transformation of the Technological Museum into the Powerhouse, and the advent of the National Maritime Museum, the Museum of Contemporary Art, the Hyde Park Barracks Museum and the Museum of Sydney. To some extent this reflects the Museum's divided commitments between research and public communication.

William Street was Sydney's most poetic street. Running east from the city to its oldest and wealthiest suburbs of Potts Point, Elizabeth Bay and Darlinghurst, William Street traversed the valley of Woolloomooloo. Between Hyde Park and the mansions at the far hill, William Street's boarding houses, hotels, pawn shops and tearooms offered welcome to all manner of strugglers—new arrivals, travellers, prostitutes, workers, petty crooks, artists and writers. During the 1880s, before he became Sydney's best-read poet, Henry Lawson lived in a William Street boarding house.

In 1916 the City Council resumed the buildings on William Street's south side, and set about creating a broad avenue. Faster access to the growing eastern suburbs was one motive; so was a desire to remove William Street's teeming masses from the sight of affluent commuters. William Street has proved resilient. The breweries rebuilt their hotels—and one heads the streetscape then and now—while the transients and bohemians steadily occupied wealthy Darlinghurst. At the head of the street, Kings Cross became their Mecca.

Sydney's main fruit and vegetable markets gave the Haymarket its name from the 1850s. An earlier occupation by potteries and kilns is remembered in the name of Brickfield Hill, from where this photo, looking north, was taken. The Haymarket was also home to numerous retailers, with Anthony Hordern and Marcus Clark building department stores. Hordern's Palace Emporium dominates this view. When completed in 1889 the Emporium was the largest department store in Sydney. Featuring one of Sydney's first passenger lifts, it was for a year or two the city's tallest building. Crowded with markets, pubs, shops and theatres, the Haymarket embodied the poet Kenneth Slessor's "truly-flavoured old Sydney, the gaslight, straw hat, bunch-of-bananas, tram-ride Sydney", of Paddy's Market and Brickfield Hill.

Hordern's Palace Emporium is long gone, destroyed in a spectacular fire in 1901. Its successor Emporium, built a few blocks further up George Street, has also vanished, replaced by office and apartment towers. With the closure of its markets and department stores during the 1960s and 1970s, the southern reach of the City was further devalued by the construction of some of Sydney's most unsightly office towers. Primarily government offices these include the McKell Building—with steps on the far right—which is the home of the NSW Government Architect's office. In the past two decades, however, Sydney's Chinese community has led a spectacular revival of the Haymarket area. Once concentrated in a few streets, Chinatown's shops, restaurants and apartments now give identity and prosperity to the Haymarket and the southern city.

Belmore Markets opened in 1893, replacing earlier fruit and vegetable market buildings on the same Haymarket site. Designed by City Architect George McRae, the new building provided stallholders with a vast unbroken floor space accessed by 36 archways to the four surrounding streets. The Markets' red brick structure was decorated with terracotta capitals, swags, keystones and roundels. Despite its size and quality, Belmore Markets was poorly sited within an increasingly busy city. Within a decade the City Council began developing markets (Paddy's Markets between Hay and Campbell) on the other side of George Street, closer to the rail yard and wharves of Darling Harbour. New produce markets were opened there in 1909.

Since ending its career as a market in 1910, Belmore Markets has been transformed more than once. It was first converted into a venue for Wirth Bros. Circus, which had been entertaining the Haymarket for some decades. The Market façade was dismantled and re-erected above a new ground floor, while an office building was added at the Pitt Street end. Reopened in 1916 as the Hippodrome, the new building featured seating for 2000, plus a circular concrete water tank for performances by seals and polar bears. The tank could be covered by a timber floor, which was used as the circus rink. In 1928, the building reopened as the Capitol Cinema and Concert Theatre, designed by Henry Eli White, who also designed the State and several other Sydney theatres. The Capitol has recently been restored and converted for theatre, with the addition of stage and wings space at its Hay Street frontage.

In 1901, work began on a new Sydney railway terminus, replacing the Redfern terminus south of the Devonshire Street Cemetery. This meant the removal of a maze of narrow streets and the old cemetery. The post-Plague resumption of more than 700 houses around the Belmore Markets enabled the creation of extensive approaches to the new station. Decorative parks and avenues were planned to connect Central Station with the city, although apart from the landscaped expanse of Belmore Park, few of these plans were fulfilled. Eddy Avenue was created between the station colonnade and Belmore Park. With the opening of Central Station in 1908, trade and transport in New South Wales was centralised. All the lines in the NSW railway network terminated at Sydney, rather than at regional centres.

The tower and upper level of Central Station were completed in the decade after 1908, obscuring the iron roof of the station concourse while creating a southern city landmark. Although electric trams carried commuters to Circular Quay and the business district, agitation increased for an underground railway which could service the city centre. The first part of the City Railway opened in 1926, with stations at St. James and Museum.

The City Railway added its railway viaduct to the two tram ramps, now in use again after a lull of some decades. With Eddy Avenue's development as an interstate bus terminal, Central Station's status as a transport gateway has been confirmed and enhanced. Mixing Neoclassicism, Australian floral motifs and massive sandstone colonnades, Central's architecture echoes the diversity of its visitors.

Australia's oldest university, the University of Sydney was established in 1850, offering an Arts degree comprising three years' study of Greek, Latin, Maths and Science. The Quadrangle is the university's signature and main building, designed by Edmund Blacket. Blacket resigned from his position as Colonial Architect when he was appointed University Architect in May 1854 for the role of designing a complex of buildings. The Quadrangle was built in the style of Medieval Gothic and influenced by Oxford and Cambridge Universities. It was not completed until the 1920s. At this time, the University appeared disconnected from the city, an impression reinforced by the fact that annual enrolments did not exceed 100 until the 1880s. New faculties of medicine, law and science increased the University's status and influence from the 1890s.

The Quadrangle complex, the enduring image of Sydney's oldest university, has been joined by a number of other buildings designed by leading architects of their day including Walter Vernon, Leslie Wilkinson and Ken Woolley. However, to this day the interior of the Great Hall with its hammer-beam roof, is still thought of as one of Australia's greatest architectural accomplishments. The University was Sydney's sole such institution until the University of New South Wales was established in the 1950s. Three other Sydney universities have since been founded—Macquarie, the University of Technology Sydney and the University of Western Sydney. From a monopoly position in students and prestige, the University of Sydney has been forced to compete in a crowded education market.

Homebush Bay was part of the area originally occupied by the Wangal people and lies inland from Sydney on the Parramatta River. In 1806, D'Arcy Wentworth received a land grant from Governor King on the west side of the bay on which he built a house called "Home Bush" on what later became the site of the State Abattoirs. Opened in 1915, it was the largest facility of its type in the Commonwealth and is the dominant feature of this photo. At their peak, the abattoirs employed 1600 people and prompted the creation of tanners and industries producing soap, dripping, oil, glue and fertiliser. Following World War II, a policy of decentralisation was adopted and the facility closed in 1988. Another landmark near the abattoirs was the State Government-owned brick-works—established in 1911 to supply government needs. Beyond can be seen the suburbs of Concord and North Strathfield.

Although some of the original buildings remain, Sydney Olympic Park has now replaced the abattoirs as the dominant feature of this area. After more than one hundred years of heavy industry the area was considered to be highly toxic. However, concern for the environment and a commitment to clean up the site ultimately helped win the bid for the successful 2000 Olympic and Paralympic Games for Sydney. Today, the park remains as a venue for sporting activities, as well as a place for people to live and work. The former Olympic Village has become one of the world's largest solar-powered suburbs. The Olympic stadium, which was the focal point of the 2000 Games, remains the major landmark in the area. All that remains of the nearby brickworks is a huge crater known as the "brickpit" that is home to a colony of rare green and yellow bell frogs.

Spectacle Island is located in the Parramatta River between Cockatoo Island and Drummoyne. Originally consisting of two small rocky islets joined by a narrow strip of land, it was named "Spectacle Island" by the Royal Navy Hydrographer in 1822 when the island was first surveyed, due to its shape resembling a pair of spectacles. Now it has been greatly altered in physical appearance—the island was entirely enclosed by a rock sea wall in 1885 and doubled in size by the dumping of both building spoil and fill brought to the island from the Balmain coal mine and from the excavation of Sutherland Dock on Cockatoo Island. The island was acquired by the RN Australian Squadron for the development of a munitions depot from the colonial government in 1860. The first building erected on the larger eastern island, between 1863 and 65, was a sandstone powder magazine designed by Colonial Architect James Barnet, followed by five other Barnet buildings, using stone mined from the island.

From 1908 until the late 1970s Spectacle Island (and its munition barges) stored munitions and maintained weapons including gun barrels and torpedoes. Supporting activities in both world wars, the Island operated at its peak during World War II when at times up to 600 people were employed there in the storage and maintenance of munitions and naval ordnance. As the munition activities reduced in the late 1970s, the Navy began transferring its Heritage Collection to the Island from storage areas around Australia.

Today, Spectacle Island continues as a naval base, its primary function being the Headquarters and Main Repository of the Naval Heritage Collection that holds some half million cultural heritage artefacts. Additionally, Australia's oldest naval cadet unit, TS Sydney, is located on the island. Spectacle Island is also used by various units of the Australian Defence Forces to conduct waterborne training on and around the island, continuing the unbroken 145-year history of Navy occupation and use of Spectacle Island.

Callan Park covers about 61 hectares (150 acres) on the southern side of Iron Cove on the Parramatta River. The area was once part of the lands of the Wangal people. The first Iron Cove Bridge was an iron lattice bridge built in 1884, when the buildings at Callan Park Hospital for the Insane were being completed. In 1873, the Colonial Government bought the estate as a site for a new lunatic asylum to be designed according to the enlightened views of the American Dr. Thomas Kirkbride. Colonial Architect James Barnet worked in collaboration with Inspector of the Insane, Dr. Frederick Norton Manning, to produce a group of some 20 Neoclassical buildings offering progressive patient care. Subsequently named the Kirkbride Block, the buildings were built of sandstone. The hospital grounds were designed by the curator of the Botanic Gardens, Charles Moore, and added to in the 1890s.

Replacement of the original Iron Cove Bridge began in 1947. The new bridge was opened in 1955 and is an outstanding example of steel truss design with many elements of Art Deco style, considered to be of State significance. The Kirkbride complex continued to be used for patients until 1994, when the last remaining services were transferred to other buildings in the expansive grounds. After massive renovations, the Sydney College of the Arts took possession in 1996. The historic sandstone buildings and courtyards have been beautifully restored and the new occupants provide a sympathetic adaptive re-use of this heritage complex. Garry Owen House, also used by Callan Park patients for many years and later as a nurses' training school, has also undergone extensive refurbishment and now houses the NSW Writers' Centre. The Callan Park Act was passed in 2002 to protect the site which is a significant historic foreshore landscape.

The largest of Sydney Harbour's islands, Cockatoo Island, is located at the meeting of the Harbour with the Parramatta and Lane Cove rivers. A jail for long-term convicts was built on the Island from 1839, and convicts cut 20 silos deep into the sandstone to store the colony's grain supply. Later, a dock and machine shop for the Royal Navy was established. After 1870, prisoners were relocated to Darlinghurst Gaol, and the Island was renamed *Biloela* (a local Aboriginal word for black cockatoo) in an attempt to remove its convict image. The industrial capacity was strengthened and shipbuilding became a major function of the Island; when completed in 1890, the Sutherland Dock was the world's largest dry dock. In 1913 the Island became the Commonwealth Naval Dockyard and the site of the construction of Australia's first steel warship, the destroyer HMAS *Huon*.

During the Pacific War, Cockatoo Island became the major dockyard for the Southern Pacific following the fall of Singapore. As well as repairing and refitting US and Australian warships, the Island reached its shipbuilding peak. However, in 1986 the supply ship HMAS *Success* became the last of 33 ships constructed at the Island for the Australian Navy. Numerous civilian freighters and liners were also launched there. The dockyard closed in 1991 and much of its equipment and fittings have been sold and removed. The island is in a state of transition having become part of the Sydney Harbour Federation Trust. As well as planned commercial maritime activity, the island is now open for tours and education, and it is being used for large-scale cultural events.

Opposite Pyrmont Point, on the Rozelle side of Johnston's Bay, Glebe Island became the receptacle for industries too noxious even for Pyrmont, Sydney's first industrial suburb. The city's main abattoirs occupied Glebe Island from the 1850s, bringing tanneries, soap and candle factories in their wake. The first Glebe Island Bridge was built during the 1850s, with a manual swing span to allow shipping into Johnston's and Rozelle Bays. It was replaced in 1901 by the short swing-span bridge pictured above. By this time, the abattoirs' smells and fouling of the harbour waters had forced its closure, although its long, low buildings can still be seen on the far Rozelle shore. The barren landscape in the photo was shortly to be transformed for deep-water wharves and railway lines.

The new Glebe Island Bridge sped development of the wharves at Rozelle and Balmain, as did the construction of the White Bay Power Station in 1917 and the grain silos in 1920. A rail link to Darling Harbour saw timber shipment become a major role of the wharves. This is now the main dock for car imports, while a third Glebe Island Bridge, the Anzac Bridge, towers over its disused predecessor. Opened in 1996, it is one of the longest concrete cable-stayed span bridges in the world and allows ample clearance for shipping, although port activity has all but ceased on its far side. Though the nearby White Bay Power Station ceased operation in 1983, its cavernous interior has found use as a cinematic location (much of *The Matrix* trilogy was filmed there) and occasional cultural venue.

Pyrmont Point was the site of Sydney's first concentration of manufacturing industry. When the Colonial Sugar Refining Company's refinery opened at the Point in 1878, its neighbours included the City Iron Works, Davy and Sands' engineering works and the shipyard of the Australasian Steam Navigation Company. CSR's refinery converted cane from Queensland and the NSW north coast to sugar and other products. In 1901 a distillery was built, producing industrial alcohol and rum, followed by the Caneite particle board factory. The CSR factories steadily expanded to occupy most of Pyrmont Point. Pyrmont was home to about 30,000 people in 1900 but its population declined thereafter as CSR and wool brokers purchased and demolished housing, replacing it with factories and wool stores. For the residents who stayed, Pyrmont was a self-contained workers' suburb.

In recent decades Pyrmont's industries have moved west and the area has been transformed through government initiative and a masterplan for dense inner city residential development. Pyrmont is now in transition to a new urban "village" and the CSR site converted into an upmarket mini-suburb, Jacksons Landing. After slumping to a population nadir of less than 2000 residents, Pyrmont's population is booming again. As the twentieth century progressed, industry spread from Pyrmont and Darling Harbour along the Parramatta River. At regular intervals the river's mangroves made way for factories producing anything from fibro to plastic. Now punctuated by these disused industrial monoliths, the foreshores' future as housing and leisure raises complex issues of heritage, environment and aesthetics as these remnants of the city's industrial past are swept away.

From its earliest days, Darling Harbour was at the centre of engineering and industrial technology. The Darling Harbour goods line, built in 1855, was one of Australia's first railways. With the expansion of the pastoral economy throughout the 1870s and 1880s the Darling Harbour yards became the major warehousing and distribution point for rural produce. In 1883 Goldsbrough Mort built a Darling Harbour wool store, the first of 20 huge wool warehouses which still dominate the streetscapes of Pyrmont and Ultimo. The eastern side of Darling Harbour was filled with finger wharves, used by the coastal shipping which brought dairy produce, timber, maize, potatoes and wool. Coastal shipping activity declined at the beginning of the twentieth century, as more goods came to Sydney by rail than ship.

Like docks all over the world, the Darling Harbour wharves were made obsolete by shipping containers. During the 1970s, a new container port was established at Botany Bay, south of the city. The railways vacated the site in 1982 and the Darling Harbour complex of parks, entertainment and retail, opened in 1988. In front of the skyscrapers on the eastern side is King Street Wharf, a combination of luxury apartments and restaurants, and Sydney's popular Aquarium. Star City dominates the western side of Darling Harbour, epitomising the harbour's shift from the functional to the frivolous. Built on the former site of Pyrmont power station, Star City features a casino, hotel, theatre and restaurants visited by up to nine million people per year.

Pyrmont Bridge opened to traffic in 1902, replacing an earlier bridge built in 1858. Designed by Percy Allan, the new structure was at the forefront of bridge technology. Its large swing span opened to allow freighters passage to the head of Darling Harbour. The swing span was powered by electricity from the new Ultimo Powerhouse, while the bridge is supported by an ingenious system of timber trusses. This "Allen Truss" system was eventually used on hundreds of bridges in Australia. The bridge was the gateway to Pyrmont's warehouses, railway yards and an international shipping terminal where cargoes of wool, grain, timber, coal and farm produce were loaded. The bridge was heavily trafficked by wool carters carrying wool to the stores and by five-and-seven horse teams from CSR and the flour mills, which crossed the bridge from Pyrmont, travelling as far as Manly to deliver goods.

The 1980s conversion of Pyrmont Bridge, from goods thoroughfare to tourist walkway, encapsulates Darling Harbour's changing role. While Sydney now retains some elements of its industrial life on the harbour, most former industrial and trading sites have been reconfigured as "lifestyle" precincts of apartments, restaurants, shops and cultural buildings. Controversially, Pyrmont Bridge was one of the few historic structures preserved at Darling Harbour. Despite the addition of the Monorail track, this oldest swing span bridge in the world grants the new precinct an element of authenticity. The Australian National Maritime Museum, designed by Sydney architect Philip Cox, dominates the left foreground of the image in a prime waterfront location, allowing for a flotilla of historic vessels to be tethered to the harbour boardwalks. It was opened by then Prime Minister, Bob Hawke, in 1991.

The Ultimo Power Station was built from 1899 to 1902 to provide power for Sydney's new electric tram system. It was one of four coal-fired power stations which blanketed the inner city with soot for much of the twentieth century—the other stations were at Pyrmont and Balmain. Containing 14 boilers, the massive boiler hall and its three chimneys are closest to the camera; the generating steam turbines were housed in the second main hall behind.

Although it also supplied power to the City Railway from the 1920s, the Ultimo Power Station ceased operation in 1963, shortly after Sydney's tram tracks were torn up. The machinery was removed and the chimneys were demolished during the 1960s and 1970s.

After standing derelict for 20 years, the Ultimo Power Station became the new home of the Museum of Applied Arts and Sciences. The museum was founded in 1880 with a collection of remnants of the Sydney International Exhibition. From 1893, the museum, then called the Technological Museum, occupied a purpose-built museum building in Ultimo, collecting in the areas of technology, decorative arts, science and history. A state-funded bicentennial project saw the museum rehoused in 1988 in the adapted Ultimo Power Station and renamed the Powerhouse Museum. With a display area of over 20,000 square metres (215,000 square feet), the Powerhouse is Australia's largest museum. It was one of the first Australian museums to embrace interactivity and other new interpretive media.

PARRAMATTA RIVER FROM FLAGSTAFF RESERVE

The green oasis of Flagstaff Hill provides an excellent vantage point to the Parramatta River, Balmain and Goat Island, and over the dense neighbourhood of nineteenth-century housing and warehousing known as Millers Point. This residential area, like the Rocks, had become problematic due to poor sanitation and population density. Not long after the photo was taken, much of the waterfront below was cleared and deep water wharves were connected directly to a broad thoroughfare, Hickson Road, and via bridges to bond stores above. Some of the houses were also resumed to make way for industrial buildings. The view takes in the Lord Nelson, one of Sydney's oldest and most historic pubs and the parapet of another pub, the Palisade, which was demolished in 1902 by the Sydney Harbour Trust to improve the physical and moral tone of the area.

A century later, the colonial sandstone Lord Nelson pub remains virtually unchanged and has become a Mecca for both tourists and Sydneysiders. The red brick Palisade on the left of the photograph, was one of the few pubs rebuilt in 1912. Walsh Bay, the name for the series of wharves built in the second decade of the twentieth century, is being returned to residential use as the obsolete wharves and warehouses are recycled as expensive harbourside housing. The wharves also house trendy new office spaces and a series of cultural facilities. Whilst much of the nineteenth century terrace housing of the area is still in public hands and the atmospheric streets remain, the area is changing to suit the demographic mix. Observatory Hill remains as an open, grassy space with panoramic views of the city, the north shore, the Parramatta River out to the west of Sydney and the southern reaches of the harbour.

Completed in 1858, Sydney Observatory was founded to establish accurate time from the movement of the stars. Correct time was especially important for ships; before setting out on a voyage, mariners adjusted the ship chronometers which enabled them to measure their longitude precisely. The time ball on the Observatory's tower was lowered everyday at 1 pm exactly. Taken about 1900, the photo captures the ball raised prior to the time signal.

The Observatory's site above Sydney Cove gave shipping a clear view of the time ball. Observatory Hill has also borne the names of Citadel Hill and Flagstaff Hill, reflecting the other purposes given this steep eminence. In 1804, Fort Phillip was constructed as a defence against convict insurrections. Part of the fort wall still stands as the platform for the signal station which, for a century from the 1820s, communicated with ships via coded flags.

Despite the practical purpose behind its foundation, the Observatory had a notable scientific career. The southern sky was largely unknown by Europeans and many of its features were first charted and photographed by the Observatory's astronomers. The Observatory also participated in international projects, notably the 1874 observations of the sun's transit in front of Venus. It also took part in a project to map and photograph the sky. The Observatory worked until 1982, retaining its original purpose for a remarkably long time. Fortunately most of its telescopes and other equipment survived, enhancing the Observatory's new role as a museum of astronomy as part of the Powerhouse Museum. The buildings and grounds have been restored to their late 1800s state and, offering a unique combination of historic, scientific and aesthetic pleasures, the Observatory is one of Sydney's most visited museums.

Windmill Street is one of the earliest (1815) streets in Millers Point, running to three windmills at the Point. The Hero of Waterloo, one of Sydney's oldest surviving pubs, was built of locally-quarried stone in 1844 by George Paton, a stonemason. With the Whaler's Arms next door and the Shipwright's Arms opposite, the Hero was one of more than 50 pubs in the area by 1880, offering accommodation and revelry to seaman and dock workers. Bubonic plague, transmitted by the fleas of infected rats which nested in the wharves and markets on the waterfront, struck these streets in January 1900. One of the most traumatic events in Sydney's history, the plague caused a quarantining of the area and 1800 of its residents. It led to many deaths, the cleansing of 4000 buildings and the demolition of many others, the removal of 105,000 tons of garbage and sewerage, and the eradication of tens of thousands of rats.

The plague forced the New South Wales government to take greater responsibility for public health and city planning. This resulted in the plague area being resumed by the government and then rebuilt. Most of the houses on Windmill Street were demolished, the land left vacant in the early photo is now occupied by a row of terrace houses, part of the first generation of public housing built in Sydney. Other existing houses were stripped and rebuilt to the standards of the time. Two doors down from the Hero of Waterloo is the Stevens Buildings, Sydney's first apartment block. Most of the buildings on the right (harbour) side of Windmill Street were also demolished and the land excavated to create a new warehouse and street below. The warehouses have since been converted to offices and other commercial uses. The Hero of Waterloo is one of only two pre-1900 hotels still serving the Millers Point area.

SUSANNAH PLACE, THE ROCKS

The Rocks was a mixture of gracious two- and three-storeyed residences and cramped cottages, pubs, shops and workshops. It was a densely-populated part of Sydney, housing working class families in close proximity to their work in an era without public transport. The bubonic plague and the slum reclamations that resulted, had a considerable effect on the area's close community with many residents displaced from their homes. The building rubble in the foreground of this photo is probably from the demolition of the buildings on the opposite side of the road as a result of the plague clearances. Susannah Place was built in 1844 and was based on English examples of terrace housing.

Susannah Place is today a rare example of a pre-1850s terrace house row, including a corner shop, that survives in the Rocks. This side of the street is little changed except for the raising of Gloucester Street to meet the approaches of the Harbour Bridge when it was constructed. Susannah Place is now below street level. The larger terrace, to the left, is public housing built for waterside workers in the 1910s after much of the plague-related demolition. Susannah Place was occupied continuously from 1844 until the late twentieth century and remains largely intact. Now a museum, the terraces are a rich record of the lives of their occupants. The site opposite is now an important archaeological site, surviving since the demolition of the buildings in the 1900s underneath various layers of use and revealed again in 1994 through extensive excavation.

The Argyle Cut was excavated to link the Rocks west of Sydney Cove with Millers Point. Two of the first areas settled in Sydney, the Rocks and Millers Point developed as separate communities, divided by the steep ridge of Observatory Hill. By the 1840s, Millers Point and Darling Harbour had developed similar warehousing and wholesaling functions as the Rocks and Sydney Cove, but the only land link between them was a circuitous trip via Kent Street. Excavation of the direct link of Argyle Cut began in 1843, using convict labour. Cutting through the sandstone ridge of the Rocks was ultimately impossible for convicts, whose slow and laborious task of hand-cutting was finally usurped with blasting the rock. The Cut was completed by City Council labourers during the 1850s. The photo depicts the view east through the Cut to Sydney Cove, beneath the Cumberland Street Bridge and Princes Street, which, like other streets in the area, was resumed for the construction of the Harbour Bridge.

The Cut was widened during construction of the Sydney Harbour Bridge. Two of its three bridges were replaced by the much broader bridge of the Bradfield Highway, carrying traffic to the Bridge. During its early decades, Argyle Cut was regarded as a dangerous area, especially during the 1880s and 1890s when the Rocks larrikin "Push" and their Millers Point rivals fought territorial contests and preyed upon pedestrians. The Cut was also portrayed in sentimental terms by photographers and artists, anxious to recapture the flavour of Australia's first residential area. Although many aspects of life in the old Rocks and Millers Point—such as daily casual hiring for work on the wharves—are not mourned, the persistence of workers' housing in the area has helped protect its character, despite the increasing presence of tourist infrastructure. At the Rocks end of the Cut, the Argyle Centre warehouse was one of the first historic structures recycled as a tourist venue.

Known by the Gamaragal (Cammerraygal) Aboriginal group as *Gorambullagong* or "peaceful waters", Mosman Bay was named by the early European settlers as Great Sirius Cove after HMS *Sirius*—the First Fleet flagship that was careened there in 1789. The bay was renamed after Archibald Mosman, a Scot who arrived in Sydney in 1828 and shortly after established a whaling station in the bay, with a stone wharf, storehouse and accommodation for his whalers. By the 1850s, shipping had moved from the bay to the maritime areas in Pyrmont and Balmain, but boat builders, boatsheds and refreshment rooms remained and ferries brought day trippers to picnic in the scenic bush. Sandstone quarried from Mosman's property by one of its subsequent owners (Richard Hayes Harnett) was used for buildings in Sydney, including the sea wall around Farm Cove. Mosman's house, "The Nest", was later demolished for residential subdivision, but the stone storehouse near the wharf survives as the Mosman Scout Hall.

Mosman Bay lies between Cremorne Point on its western edge and Curraghbeena Point on its east in close proximity to the city of Sydney by water. It is graced with natural beauty and blessed with harbour foreshore access, with a number of reserves around its perimeter. Residential development of the area began with the first land sale in 1874, and by 1893 Mosman was declared a separate municipality. Much development occurred after 1900 and the area retains a great deal of its Federation and Edwardian architecture, although close proximity to the city and ferry access has encouraged higher density accommodation in the form of apartment blocks. Mosman Wharf today stands on wooden piles above the original stone wharf. From the wide promenade leading to the wharf there is a pleasant view across the marina to the Mosman Rowing Club. The view beyond is to the wealthy residential area of Cremorne Point and beyond that to the city with a glimpse of the Harbour Bridge.

Governor Arthur Phillip first visited Manly in 1788 and named the cove after the manly bearing of the Aboriginal men he saw there. Manly's development owes much to Henry Gilbert Smith, an entrepreneur who started a ferry service there in 1854, running the iron paddle-steamers *Victoria*, *Emu* and *Black Swan*. Realising Manly's potential as a seaside resort, Smith built a pier, the Pier Hotel, and a picturesque main thoroughfare, named 'the Corso' after a street in Rome. Hoping to attract permanent residents, Smith also bought up land, which he subdivided in 1855 to create a township. The ferry service expanded and the Port Jackson Steam Boat Company was incorporated in 1877, becoming the Port Jackson and Manly Steamship Company in 1907. The company auctioned land in Manly and offered free five-year ferry passes to those who built homes in the area, hoping to create a permanent commuting population to offset the weekend excursionists.

The Port Jackson and Manly Steamship Company continued its role in the development of Manly; building hot and cold saltwater baths, tearooms and, in 1933, the "wonder pool" for the benefit of the hordes of day-trippers who came by ferry from Sydney. Manly has become increasingly urbanised and a much sought-after address for Sydneysiders. The spectacular views and proximity to water has contributed to the growth of apartment buildings in the area in the twentieth century. Houses jostle with three- and four-storey walk-ups and apartment towers from the 1960s and 1970s along with more recent buildings which now loom over the suburb. The ferry and Jetcat are still patronized by residents of Manly as a convenient way to reach the city and by tourists, with the ferry trip to Manly an essential part of the tourist's itinerary. The seaside suburb boasts a number of attractions, including an aquarium, a museum and art gallery and areas of safe swimming.

Because of the reef and island in the bay, Coogee's surf is generally moderate compared to that of most Sydney beaches. This may be why it developed something of the character of the English seaside. Coogee became a successful resort before Bondi. In 1887 the domed Palace Aquarium opened at the north end of the beach. With pleasure gardens, sea water baths, dance hall and restaurants, Coogee attracted large weekend crowds. In 1928 an amusement pier—similar to those found at many English resorts—was built. Commencing at the promenade it reached over 180 metres (591 feet) into the sea, next to a shark-proof swimming enclosure. Floodlights permitted night surfing, and for a few years Coogee was Sydney's most popular beach, attracting tens of thousands of swimmers on summer nights. In 1934, however, the pier was demolished after sustaining storm damage; Coogee's heyday had passed.

During the 1980s the Coogee seafront was redeveloped, although the beach esplanade pictured in Charles Kerry's photo remains. The Coogee Bay Hotel, the oldest resort hotel at Coogee, was extended, part of a boom in new holiday accommodation. Coogee has since become a favourite with "backpacker" tourists. Perhaps the major change since the 1900s is reflected in the clothing worn on the esplanade. Suits and other items of Sunday best are rarely encountered, while the creation of surfwear and other elements of surf culture is arguably the most notable Australian achievement in the field of popular culture. The Palace Aquarium building still dominates the beach's northern end, although it now houses a shopping and restaurant complex. The building retains a certain notoriety from a murder case, initiated in 1935 after an Aquarium shark disgorged the severed arm of a murdered criminal.

Development of Bondi began at the south end of the beach—spurred by the extension, in 1887, of a tramline to the bottom of Bondi Road. By 1900 the tramline had been extended again to the middle of the beach, where it ended in a balloon loop. By this time a number of hotels were operating in the area and housing had begun to follow the progression of the tramline. Victorian moralists viewed surf bathing as an unseemly exposure of near-naked bodies.

By the 1880s, public bathing was banned at Sydney beaches between the hours of 9am and 8pm, restricting the activity to the early part of the day. Swimming in harbour pools was usually segregated at this time. Clothed waders have the surf to themselves in Henry King's beach photo. Public disobedience and police inactivity rendered the law redundant, and by 1900 the first surf lifesaving clubs had been formed.

The shape of Bondi Beach has remained largely unchanged since 1929. In that year the Bondi Beach Improvement Scheme was completed. The sea wall at the back of the beach was consolidated into a marine drive; parklands were established and the Bondi Pavilion was built. Several hotels and numerous apartment blocks were built around Bondi Beach during the 1920s as well. During the 1950s and 1960s Bondi became a boisterously plebeian suburb, home to several workers' clubs. One of these—the Bondi Icebergs Winter Swimming Club—that can be seen at the southern end of the beach, was formed in 1929 by lifesavers who wanted to swim year round. The Icebergs Club has, in the past decade, been made over in a more glamorous style, rather like Bondi in general. Sydney's current self-image, as a combination of world city and beach resort, is based in part on the fame of Bondi Beach.

The Macquarie Lighthouse commands a significant place in Australia's maritime history. Since the erection of a signal flagstaff in 1791, there has been a navigational aid on this site on the cliffs south of the entrance to Sydney Harbour. The oldest serving lighthouse in Australia, the Macquarie light was designed by Francis Greenway and completed in 1818.

Greenway warned that the lighthouse was built with poor-quality sandstone, but despite steady deterioration, the lighthouse was not replaced until 1882 when a stronger tower was built next to it. Designed by Colonial Architect James Barnet, the foundation stone was laid in 1880. The lighthouse was built as a replica of the former lighthouse, which was demolished in 1883, but included a larger lantern and apparatus.

Despite the Lighthouse's presence, shipwrecks remained a hazard. South Head's worst catastrophe occurred in 1857, when the clipper Dunbar smashed against the cliffs; all but one of the 122 people on board perished.

The lighting apparatus, described as the most efficient in the world for its time, was electric in operation. One of the generators is displayed at the Lighthouse, as well as the original switchboard. In clear weather the light was provided by a gas burner, with the electric apparatus only used in bad weather. However, the new light was too expensive to operate and the lighthouse did not use electricity continuously until 1933, when the city power supply was connected. By 1976 the lighthouse was fully automated, but the last lighthouse keepers stayed on until 1989. The first lighthouse keeper was Robert Watson, the former quartermaster of HMS *Sirius*, the First Fleet flagship.

The heritage landscape of the area has been restored, with elements including the driveway, gate piers, gates and fencing reconstructed to Barnet's original design.

Watsons Bay was named after Robert Watson, quartermaster of HMS *Sirius*. Watson received a land grant on the peninsular from Governor King in the early 1800s and was the first superintendent of the Macquarie Lighthouse. Watsons Bay's transition from a fishing village to a tourist destination began when the first hotels were established there in the 1850s, attracting day-trippers and holiday-makers from the city. The large estates in the Watsons Bay area were subdivided later than in other Sydney suburbs, and the district was slow to experience the commuter demands which come with residential development. A regular ferry service ran to Watsons Bay from the 1870s, carrying both residential and tourist traffic. Tourists were catered to by the Palace Hotel, built around 1886, and the Ozone Tea Rooms.

By 1909 the ferries had to compete with the extended tram service which ran along New South Head Road. The service was discontinued in 1933, although today the ferry runs again to Watsons Bay. Refreshment rooms were built on the Watsons Bay ferry pier in 1904, and run for three generations by the Marinato family, whose descendants still live in Watsons Bay. The Bay has since become a favourite spot for seafood, enjoyed with spectacular views of the harbour and the city skyline from the long-established Doyle's restaurant on the pier and in the Watson's Bay Hotel. A less happy Watsons Bay feature is "The Gap", a steep drop from the ocean cliffs behind the Bay and village. Situated near the bus and tram terminus, the Gap was for many years a preferred suicide spot for the depressed and desperate.

This area was home to some of the wealthiest free-settler residents in nineteenth-century Sydney who took advantage of land grants on Woolloomooloo Hill (now called Potts Point). The house sites were chosen for their vistas across Sydney harbour and reflected the rise of the detached villa, set within several acres of landscaped garden, as the ideal form of middle-class housing. Many of the houses built on Woolloomooloo Hill were built as Greek Revival villas. One of the most elegant and sophisticated houses of the area is Elizabeth Bay House. Built between 1835 and 1839, Elizabeth Bay House was known as "the finest house in the colony". Designed by the most fashionable and accomplished architect of the day, John Verge, for the Colonial Secretary, Alexander Macleay and his family, Elizabeth Bay House is a superb example of colonial architecture. The house was once surrounded by an extensive 22 heactare (54 acre) garden and described as a "botanist's paradise".

The contemporary view projects a radically different urban picture. Long gone are most of the grand nineteenth-century colonial and Victorian residences. They have been replaced by successive apartment booms. Art Deco and Spanish Mission apartments from the 1920s and 1930s and functionalist cream and red brick apartments of the 1960s now jostle with an array of contemporary, upmarket, architect-designed apartment blocks. Retaining a bohemian feel, the area provides an attractive urban scale with a large collection of cafés and galleries for residents and others visiting the area. Elizabeth Bay House, now managed by Historic Houses Trust of NSW, remains but is now dwarfed by surrounding apartment buildings. The area also boasts one of Sydney's most expensive houses, "Boomerang". Shrouded in trees at the water's edge, it was designed in 1926 by Neville Hampson, apparently inspired by Randolph Hearst's Castle at San Simeon in California.

Until the 2000 Olympics, the 1908 world heavyweight title fight between Jack Johnson and Tommy Burns was the most famous sporting event to be held in Sydney. About 25,000 people crowded into the outdoor stadium, constructed for the occasion at Rushcutter's Bay by the fight's promoter, Hugh D. McIntosh. McIntosh succeeded in luring the champion, Burns, into a title defence against his black American challenger, Johnson. American and European promoters enforced a sporting 'colour bar' and refused to give Johnson his chance. In Sydney, Johnson easily defeated Burns. The first black world champion, Johnson returned to the USA, where he defeated a succession of "great white hopes". The Kerry photo sees Johnson, Burns and entourages in the ring shortly before the fight. The houses of Paddington form the background, with the tower of Paddington Town Hall crowning the ridge.

McIntosh's stadium by New South Head Road was soon converted to a smaller, enclosed venue. It was demolished in 1970 to make way for the railway bridge of the new Eastern Suburbs line. Known as the "Tin Shed" for its iron roof and walls, the stadium was Sydney's main entertainment venue for decades, hosting touring performers from Gene Krupa and Johnny Ray, to the Beatles and Bob Dylan. The neighbouring White City tennis complex survives, but has also lost its place in Sydney's sporting hierarchy, replaced by a new Tennis Centre at Olympic Park, Homebush. In the distance is the ridge of Paddington—one of Sydney's oldest inner city suburbs, which retains much of its terrace housing from the nineteenth century.

By the 1820s Sydney was in desperate need of a new gaol. The Sydney Gaol on George Street was overcrowded, but there was disagreement concerning both the location and the design of a new gaol. Work on the perimeter walls began in 1822 using convict labour, but had ceased by 1824 and did not then recommence until 1836 when the Committee appointed by Governor Bourke finally adopted a design. It was published over the joint signatures of the Colonial Architect, Mortimer Lewis, and the commanding Royal Engineer in Sydney—Captain George Barney.

The plan of the Gaol was influenced by the designs of the Society for the Improvement of Prison Discipline and other recent gaols in England and America. The Gaol was first occupied in an incomplete state in June 1841.

Darlinghurst Gaol remained the main Sydney penitentiary until its inmates were transferred to the new Long Bay Complex.

Darlinghurst Gaol was famously written about by the poet Henry Lawson in his poem *One-Hundred-and-Three* published in 1908. Lawson had been incarcerated there on several occasions for petty offences, including non-payment of alimony.

The photo shows the Chapel, which has recently been restored and is used for exhibitions and functions by the National Art School. It was formerly the Gaol Chapel. Darlinghurst Gaol had witnessed over 70 executions, including the bushranger "Captain Moonlight" and the last woman to hang in NSW, Louisa Collins, and had also been used as an internment camp during World War I.

In 1921, the site was transferred to the Department of Education and converted as the East Sydney Technical College. In that same year the National Art School was moved there and remains there today as an independent and highly regarded fine arts institution.

Sandwiched between the Domain and the wealthy ridges of Darlinghurst and Potts Point, Woolloomooloo in 1901 was a densely-built warren of terrace houses, mostly small, basic and already 50 years or more old. They were tenanted by a working class community employed on the harbour's wharves, sawmills and timber yards. Woolloomooloo Bay is shown shortly before the construction, in 1910, of the largest of Sydney's finger wharves. These "cathedrals of commerce" were some of the largest timber-framed structures ever constructed. Clad with a mosaic of timber, iron and asbestos sheeting, Sydney's finger wharves are among the most distinctive of Sydney's structures. Harbour pools are another Sydney institution, and a succession of pools has occupied the same Woolloomooloo Bay site since the 1820s. Now named the Andrew "Boy" Charlton pool, after a 1920s swimming champion, the current baths was redeveloped to a design by Ed Lippmann and re-opened in 2002.

The Woolloomooloo finger wharf was central to the thriving industrial and maritime city until the 1970s, when its function was usurped by the container ports and cheap air travel. It was also the site of departure and arrival of troops to the two world wars of the twentieth century. The wharf remained in a state of decay until 1987, when the NSW Government decided to demolish it to make way for a marina. After years of negotiation, public outcry and a union "green ban" of the wharf's demolition, the Government agreed to redevelop the site. It has since become an upmarket hotel and apartments with a series of cafés and restaurants and a public walkway along the water's edge. Similar controversies marked the redevelopment of Woolloomooloo during the 1970s. Originally marked for redevelopment as an office precinct, Woolloomooloo's townscape was redeveloped for public housing. More exclusive residences crowd the Darlinghurst ridge to the east.

Sydney's public art gallery was established in the early 1870s and moved to its present site, overlooking the harbour, in 1885. Although leading architects vied for the job of creating a permanent replacement for the temporary "art barn", the Gallery was eventually designed by Government Architect Walter Liberty Vernon. Despite his Gothic and Arts and Crafts tastes, Vernon followed the Gallery Trustees' preference for a Grecian Classical façade and portico, now well-loved features of the Domain. This 1914 photo shows Court 9, now used for the Australian collection, hung with European works. In the corner are two art students at their easels. The copying of Old Masters and other works was a standard part of art training and the gallery was regularly used for this purpose. The vast skylights were the only lighting until electricity was introduced in the 1930s.

Most of the Gallery's early collection is now displayed in the galleries occupying the southern half of the building, designed by Vernon and opened between 1897 and 1901. These galleries include the Paris Salon paintings and the nineteenth century Australian Collections that remain popular with visitors. The size of the Art Gallery more than doubled with new extensions completed in 1972 and during each succeeding decade. A spectacular Asian Gallery is the most recent addition, cementing the Art Gallery's status as Sydney's leading museum, whether measured in terms of visitation or cultural profile. Both the 1972 and 1987 additions, by Andrew Andersons, won the Sulman prize for architecture. A busy programme of temporary exhibitions contributes to this eminence, as does the expanded display of the Gallery's permanent collection.

In 1851 a cricket ground was marked out near the Victoria Barracks for the use of British soldiers quartered there. Initially known as the Military and Civil Ground, the field was upgraded in 1877 at the suggestion of the NSW Cricket Association. Since then, the ground has been Sydney's main cricket venue, although it has also hosted a surprising variety of sports, including tennis, cycling, athletics, baseball, rugby, rugby league, football and Australian rules football. The photograph was taken in February 1895, during the fourth match of one of the early Test series against England. Australia won this match comfortably, although England triumphed in the series. At this time only the Members Stand and two other stands had been built, and most spectators lounged on the broad expanse of the grassed "Hill" at the Randwick end of the ground.

In the century or so between the two photos, a mechanical scoreboard was built above the Hill, later replaced by an electronic board. The Hill itself is gone, buried beneath bleacher seating. Apart from the Members Pavilion and the Ladies Stand at the Paddington end, little remains of the Cricket Ground's historic character. Some of the early stands, notably the 1895 Bob Stand, were removed to suburban ovals. Over time they have been replaced by a variety of structures as the grounds have endeavoured to adapt to modern needs. In 1988, the Sydney Football Stadium was opened at the city end of the Cricket Ground. Designed by Philip Cox, this spectacular structure set a new standard for Australian sports architecture. It also relieved the Cricket Ground of the responsibility of hosting sports other than cricket and Australian football.

Centennial Park played a central role in Australian Federation on 1 January 1901. On a hot January Sydney day, this plaster and timber pavilion hosted the inauguration of the union of six British colonies to form the Federation of Australia.

The pavilion was one of numerous temporary decorative structures erected throughout Sydney for the Federation celebrations. Designed by Government Architect Walter Liberty Vernon, the Federation Pavilion combined native floral motifs with imperial symbols, including the reclining lions at each corner. The pavilion underlined the partial nature of Australia's new independence.

In 1811 Governor Macquarie had designated the area as the Second Sydney Common after Hyde Park. The park remained undeveloped until the 1880s, when Charles Moore, Director of the Botanic Gardens, recruited hundreds of unemployed men to turn the native scrub, creeks and sandy soil into a massive urban park in the European tradition, with formal gardens, ponds, statues and grand avenues.

One hundred years on, Centennial Park continues to play a critical role as a vital green space in the rapidly growing city of Sydney.

The Federation pavilion surmounted a hexagonal granite memorial called the Commonwealth Stone. Its plaster in disrepair, the pavilion was removed in 1903, leaving the stone unadorned until a new Federation Pavilion was opened as part of the 1988 celebrations to mark the bicentenary of European settlement.

Designed by Sydney architect Alec Tzannes, the new Federation Pavilion is surrounded by a sandstone colonnade beneath a copper clad domed roof. While classically-inspired like its predecessor, the new structure subtly distorts the proportions and meanings of Classicism. The interior of the dome was designed by artist Imants Tiller, with 1440 vitreous enamelled-steel panels creating a mosaic of Australian society and culture.

The questioning message of the new Pavilion is summarised in the words of its encircling frieze: “Mammon or Millennial Eden”, words from Bernard O'Dowd's 1901 sonnet “Australia”.

INDEX